# UNTO THE AGES OF AGES

## PRAISE FOR *UNTO THE AGES OF AGES*

Sebastian Morello's *Unto the Ages of Ages* is a deeply thoughtful set of reflections about Catholicism, Conservatism and England in the twenty-first century. Morello distrusts ideology and abstraction, and defends a piety of love, family and particular connection. This is philosophy through experience and history. Morello's enemies — the fake, the ugly, the intellectually vulgar — will be your enemies too.

— **DR THOMAS PINK**, Emeritus Professor of Philosophy, King's College London

In *Unto the Ages of Ages*, Sebastian Morello delivers a ferocious defence of tradition, urging a return to the sacred roots of community and culture amidst secular decay. He dissects and dismantles a dizzying array of the many and various conceptual idols scattered across the wastelands of modernity. Brimming with arresting reflections on family, faith, and folkways, these essays meld philosophical depth, practical wisdom, and political acumen in a manner few other writers today can achieve. Morello's clarion call for a God-centred conservatism offers hope and clarity to those of us who yearn for meaning and order in our fractured world.

— **DR JAMES ORR**, Associate Professor of Philosophy of Religion, University of Cambridge

This is a book unafraid to go where many others fear to tread — undertaking 'the hard slog of retrieving a pre-modern mind and heart' in the political realm, and working admirably against the tide of today's seemingly endless corruptions and false turns.

— **DR JACOB PHILLIPS**, Professor of Systematic Theology, St Mary's University, Twickenham

Sebastian Morello has emerged as one of our finest writers and thinkers on all the things that matter most to mankind, and yet are strangely most beleagued and betrayed: home, country, friendship, worship, God. Reading his essays is a refreshing draught from a limpid stream of insight and courage; these pages flow with rigorous arguments made whole by deeply-felt sentiment.

—**DR PETER A. KWASNIEWSKI**, *Tradition and Sanity*

Many writers of a 'Conservative' or 'Traditional' bent are quite clear as to what they oppose, but are rather vague as to what they favour. Others seek to separate political from religious questions, and still more are ready to accept the present regime as the best we are likely to get, simply advocating alterations of its most egregious features. In this book, Sebastian Morello falls into none of these traps. Instead, he offers an enthralling, encompassing vision, deeply rooted in the Catholic Faith, seeking to convert—not merely accept—what passes for Modernity. Nor is he what might be called defensive—he sees the struggle today for what it ultimately is: a spiritual battle, and one between good and evil. As you will see in these pages, it is a battle he means for all of us to win.

—**CHARLES COULOMBE**, author of *The Compleat Monarchist*

# UNTO THE AGES OF AGES

## ✿ ESSAYS ✿
### *on*
### *Political Traditionalism*

## SEBASTIAN MORELLO

*Foreword by Ben Reinhard*
*Afterword by Nina Power*

AROUCA
PRESS

Published by Arouca Press in cooperation
with *The European Conservative*.

© 2025 by Sebastian Morello
Waterloo, ON N2J 0A5
www.aroucapress.com

ISBN: 978-1-998492-49-7 (pbk)
ISBN: 978-1-998492-50-3 (hc)
ISBN: 978-1-998492-51-0 (ebook)

Cover design: Julian Kwasniewski

*Dedication*
To the "Tooting Fratelli," Pierpaolo and Theo,
with whom many of the ideas herein were shaped.

# CONTENTS

FOREWORD *by Ben Reinhard*  xiii

ACKNOWLEDGEMENTS  xix

INTRODUCTION  xxi

⚜ PART I: *For the Love of Home*  1

  1. The Human Person is Endangered  3

  2. The Need for Nostalgia  10

  3. The Modern State Will Become Very Religious  17

  4. Patriotism and National Identity  26

  5. Against a National Loyalty Divorced
     from the Sacred  35

  6. Christians Should Welcome Stricter
     Border Controls  41

⚜ PART II: *England and its Neighbour*  49

  1. Delaying the End of England:
     On Entering the Little Platoons  51

  2. Common Culture and Identity:
     On Surviving as a People  56

  3. England's Conservatism and the
     Global Revolution  64

  4. The Tragedy of the Sarum Rite  70

  5. Sacré-Cœur Basilica:
     Counter-Revolution Incarnate  76

  6. Abortion as a French Constitutional Right  80

⚜ PART III: *Tradition and Revolution*  87

  1. Ten Traditionalist Principles for
     the Political Struggle  89

  2. Libertarian "Conservatism": A Trojan Horse  98

  3. Conservatism's Generational Divide  104

4. Liberalism's Pathological Aversion to Suffering 111

5. Criminalising "Conversion Therapy" in
   a Liberal Democracy 119

6. Midwits: The True Enemies of
   Counter-Revolution 123

7. Should We Call Ourselves Conservatives? 129

PART IV: *Breaking Free by Binding Ourselves* 137

1. Towards a Right-Wing Ecumenism 139
   Burke, Maistre, and Solovyov 139

2. F·R·I·E·N·D·S: A Work of Truly
   Bewitching Propaganda 145

3. Folk Music and Dancing with Children 151

4. On Not Looking Awful 157

AFTERWORD *by Nina Power* 163

INDEX OF NAMES 173

*We could say that modern culture is a disputation of principles, a distortion, a twisting, and a reversal—but of what? Of Tradition, that most powerful foundation of all mankind that ensured its survival and flourishing for millennia. Returning to Tradition is not as impossible as it might seem.*

*In the conditions of the modern world, any stubborn and desperate resistance, any uncompromising struggle against liberalism, globalism, and Satanism, is heroism.*

*When the dead pass away, their earthly energies remain in the world. If you were wise, you could invite them in. If you were very wise, you could embody their will. Arise, o dead!*

—Daria Platonova Dugina

# ❧ FOREWORD ❧

*Stand by the roads, and look,*
*and ask for the ancient paths*
*where the good way is; and walk in it,*
*and find rest for your souls*
— Jeremiah 6:16

WHILE IT IS UNWISE TO PRESUME TOO much understanding of Divine Providence, it does seem that God sends each age the guides it most desperately needs. This is, in retrospect, easy enough to discern in history. To consider only the events of the last century: the dark days of 1939–1945 witnessed the rise of the great Christian humanists—men like C.S. Lewis, T.S. Eliot, and Christopher Dawson—who provided the Western world with the imaginative and intellectual resources it needed to survive the crisis of World War II, and to navigate the peace afterwards. By contrast, the long and transformative post-war years gave us gentler figures—the Roger Scrutons and Russell Kirks—who, had we but listened, might have restrained the West from its headlong rush into an ever-more rapacious individualism, and restored to it the spiritual principles necessary for its flourishing. Today, as we witness the rapid collapse of late modernity (less painful than the great wars, but no less cataclysmic), we see the beginnings of a new conservative movement. The name of this movement is unimportant (call it anti-liberal or counterrevolutionary or radical, or whatever you will); the truth that drives it is clear. The old neoliberal consensus is dead, its leading advocates increasingly tired, shrill, and inconsequential. All the energy and verve—and all the interesting voices—are now found on the other side. Such is the voice of Sebastian Morello.

I no longer remember what first drew me, as an American academic, to *The European Conservative*, or which of Morello's writings I first encountered there. I do remember, however, what came shortly after: the surprise at finding the

same name in the byline of its most interesting articles, and
the inescapable conclusion that Morello was the soundest and
clearest-sighted critic in the pages of that excellent journal. It
is therefore a joy to see many of his best articles of political
thought and social criticism collected in a single volume and
made available to a broader audience. These essays, though
wide-ranging in their scope, are bound together by a unifying theme; this beating heart of Morello's philosophy can
be expressed in only a few sentences. Rejecting the modern
paradigm of the pre-social "authentic individual," Morello
insists that the invaluable and irreplaceable human person
emerges from community:

> Human beings actualise their *personhood* precisely
> by being inducted into the communities from
> which they have come, with their histories, cul-
> tures, laws, and customs. Via this process, people
> cease to be slaves to ignorance and appetite, and
> they discover their *personal* freedom.

We are invited, then, to recognize that freedom is found not
in self-indulgence or self-actualization (often, as J. R. R. Tolkien observed, two names for the same thing), only in adherence to tradition, community, and the Permanent Things.

To the unwary, this may seem like a simple claim. And
perhaps it is; but then, so was the claim that the earth
revolves around the sun. Accepting it changes everything.
Morello's account of the human person is the fulcrum of
a lever that can move the whole world: not only how we
vote, but also the more important questions of how we
form our communities, spend our free time, and educate
our children — and even, perhaps surprisingly, how we dress.
True nostalgia is here in abundance; escapism, not at all.
There is a hard-edged practicality to Morello's argument:
he reminds his readers that they are born into this moment
and must work out their salvation within it. How we do so
is of the highest importance. Where some critics advocate a
quasi-quietist withdrawal and others see nothing wrong in
accepting the governing paradigm, Morello rightly recognizes

that neither option is viable. Rather, he tells us that the "Christian religion and the mission to establish Christendom are . . . inseparable." Transformation — of souls, families, and that family of families, the nation — is necessary.

It is difficult to overstate how urgently needed this message is. The myth of the infinitely malleable, atomised, authentic self — and the acceptance of the technocratic paradigm necessary to achieve it — is the great lie of the modern age, infecting even those minds who should most certainly know better. The very week I received this book, I heard some students (bright, committed, and devout Catholic students) argue that it is better to live in the anti-Catholic anti-culture of late modernity than in the more integrated Christian cultures of the past. In the old days, they told me, people were mere *cultural* Christians and their religion shallow and insubstantial; today's Catholics, by contrast, possess a voluntarily chosen and therefore sincere and authentic faith. The temporal flourishing and final destiny of the faithless masses seem not to have concerned them; nor did the prospect of raising children in the spiritual and moral equivalent of a radioactive wasteland. That their *own* faith might be compromised by the acceptance of presuppositions antithetical to it seems to have registered not at all. Alas, this is perhaps to be expected. Morello argues — occasionally in this volume, and more thoroughly in others — that the modern world has become quite literally *spellbound*, ensorcelled by the dark enchantment of modernity. To read *Unto the Ages of Ages*, and grapple with its arguments, may be the beginning of a liberation. The first step, after all, is to admit you have a problem.

As he pursues this project of liberation, Morello exhibits a clarity of perception and a generosity of spirit that distinguishes him from the great mass of conservative-minded critics today. He eschews the lazy, clichéd, and superficial critique characteristic of online discourse; he never descends to simple abuse. This does not mean, however, that he avoids the pressing issues. Thus, like many critics of our epoch, Morello grapples with the phenomenon of "wokeness"; unlike the overwhelming majority, he does not content himself with mocking its myriad absurdities and excesses. Instead, he exhibits an almost Dawsonian sensitivity to the humane and spiritual crises that have given the movement its urgency:

> I remain unconvinced that we have diagnosed "woke" properly. We should see it for what it is, *namely an expression of a very deep and noble religious need*, a need that has been neglected and mistreated in contemporary British society and everywhere secularism has become the dominant social and political paradigm. (emphasis mine).

Indeed, because they recognize the religious nature of man, the Woke may well be closer to the truth than the complacent representatives of the Establishment, whether on the Right or Left, who neglect it. The goal therefore must be not simply to defeat the Woke at the ballot box — and still less to mock them into online oblivion — but to offer a more coherent and satisfying vision of human flourishing. The 1990s are, after all, dead and buried. We cannot defeat the movement born out of irreligious secularism by a revival of irreligious secularism. Only a return to true religion will do. Without this return, the root causes of the Woke revolution will remain untreated, and recent conservative victories will prove fleeting: nothing more than minor detours on the road to a more crushing, and perhaps final, defeat.

It is of course impossible (and undesirable!) to deliver a comprehensive program of spiritual renewal within the pages of a book. But Morello admirably introduces his readers to the habits of thought, thinkers (Edmund Burke, Joseph de Maistre, John Henry Newman), and real-world activities (ancient liturgies, little platoons, care for the land) necessary to make such renewal possible. In this way, reading *Unto the Ages of Ages* feels almost like an initiation — or, better, as the intellectual preparation for an initiation that can only take place in the real world.

Restoring the moral and spiritual vision of a people is a monumental task in any nation and any age. For all this, a special word of introduction may need to be directed to Morello's American readers — who, it is to be hoped, will be numerous. American social conservatives have long used Europe in general, and England in particular, as a kind of cultural foil: an example of what may happen here, should our vigilance fail. At its best, these comparisons serve as a sober call to action; at worst, as the occasion for a complacent and parochial smugness. The American reader who approaches Morello's essays in this spirit will admittedly find much to confirm his presuppositions. England's nearly unrivalled surveillance state and its criminalization of "conversion therapy"; its reckless madness for immigration and its effective disenfranchising of its Christian majority — they're all here, displayed and diagnosed with generous spirit and clinical precision. Americans can learn from this example and be grateful that England's crises are not our crises, nor its vices our vices.

But if England's vices are not our vices, neither are its virtues our virtues: and here we find this book's particular profit for the American reader. To read Morello's almost lyrical praise of his native land is to be reminded of what we Americans have lost — or, perhaps, never had in the first place. The supra-rational and humane English countryside, with its copses and hedgerows and footpaths; the deeply embedded folk culture that still endures in isolated pockets; the sacred landscape that preserves the memory of a millennium of prayer and personal holiness: all these are absent in America, and (as the product of centuries) not easily replicable in the New World. Yet this detritus of ages is, as Morello shows, the civilizational leaf-mould from which all cultural growth emerges. Morello contemplates conservatism in the land of Bede and Chaucer, Shakespeare and Burke, Newman and Chesterton; American readers would do well to reflect on what living tradition should look like in the land of the interstate highway, the Walmart Supercenter, and Amazon Prime. We might find that the answer asks more of us than we might expect.

Similarly, when Morello turns his gaze to America's *own* special vices — most pointedly, the poisonous pop culture that we take in with the air we breathe, and in turn have exported to the farthest reaches of the globe — we may find ourselves squirming under his inspection. In 1943, the prophetic Tolkien worried that the victory of the terrifying "Americo-cosmopolitanism" might be — on the intellectual and spiritual plane — as bad or worse "for the world as a whole and in the long run" than the victory of Nazi Germany.[1] But American cosmopolitanism *did* win — and Morello's post-mortem on the American empire of liberalism largely confirms Tolkien's fears.

The day is far spent. How then should we live? Though the situation sketched by Morello is dire, none of this should be understood as a counsel of lethargy or futility. Once again, Morello shows that we are called not to despair, nor to endless and fruitless argument, but to action: personal, familial, communal, and national. It is the only way. As Dante demonstrated centuries ago, the breakdown of the commonwealth naturally coincides with increasingly vicious sins in the populace: pride and envy, wrath and sloth. Arguing on the internet can be fun — and, for some, it may even be profitable. Anxiety and despair, though unpleasant, at least demand nothing from their hosts. Such activities, alas, only feed the beast. More is asked of us. "You must change your life," wrote Rainer Maria Rilke. Reading *Unto the Ages of Ages*, I was left with the same conviction. And this is perhaps the highest praise I can lavish on this volume. It is impossible to read Morello's essays through with full comprehension without hearing a call to conversion. *You must change your life.* The author has done his job: it now falls to the reader to do his.

Dr. Ben Reinhard, Professor of English
*Franciscan University of Steubenville*
*March 2025*

---

[1] J. R. R. Tolkien, "Letter 53," in *The Letters of J. R. R. Tolkien*, ed. Humphrey Carpenter (London: HarperCollins, 2012), 65.

# ❧ ACKNOWLEDGEMENTS ❧

MY DEEPEST GRATITUDE TO MARIO AND Ellen Fantini, in whose wonderful journal, *The European Conservative*, much of what became the content of this volume first appeared. My thanks to Pierpaolo Finaldi and Theo Howard—to whom these collected essays are dedicated—for the many conversations that helped to develop numerous ideas now found in this book, and for the important friendship that formed the context of those conversations.

A very special thanks to Ben Reinhard who wrote the Foreword to this work; he is, it is clear, truly a kindred spirit over the Pond. And my thanks in equal measure to the author of this book's Afterword, Nina Power, whose character mystically combines the qualities of tender inspirer and shieldmaiden.

My thanks to John Rao for his work at the Roman Forum and to all involved in this scholarly community, which has gone from strength to strength since the great Dietrich von Hildebrand founded it nearly six decades ago. The intellectual and spiritual profit I have made on account of belonging to this faculty for over a decade far exceeds any contribution I have made to it.

My thanks to Joseph Shaw, Tim O'Callaghan, and all those who have been involved in running with me the Iota Unum lectures in London under the auspices of the Latin Mass Society of England and Wales. Many fascinating speakers and attendees have been present at these lectures, and consequently much interesting discussion has ensued, especially on the topics of our religious and cultural heritage and the turbulent question of the so-called "Church-state relation." These occasions have undoubtedly made their mark on my thought.

I am grateful for the support and friendship especially of Declan and Marie Jones, Clive Watson, James Bogle, Francis and Annabel Osborn, George Carter, Peter and Marie

Jones, Thomas and Judy Pink, Mary Harrington, Charles Coulombe, and Dominic and Aoife Jones. A special thanks also to Harrison Pitt, who edited many of the initial drafts of what became the chapters of this book. Of course, I remain perpetually grateful to my mentor Roger Scruton. And my very profoundest gratitude to my wife and children, to my parents, and to my brothers and their families.

Finally, many thanks to Alex Barbas and the team at Arouca Press for publishing this volume and exercising such heroic patience towards me.

# ✦ INTRODUCTION ✦

THE TITLE OF THIS BOOK, "UNTO THE Ages of Ages" is of course the vernacularisation of a term that appears repeatedly in the Holy Scriptures and in the liturgies of the Church Universal, in the Latin rites: *In Saecula Saeculorum*. It is from such Latin words that we also get a term whose meaning has been outstandingly corrupted in modernity, namely "secular." Today, we tend to think of the *secular* as being distinct from the *sacred* insofar as it denotes the "non-religious." This, however, is nonsense. There is no such thing as the "non-religious." All reality of which we have experience is contingent on non-contingent Being. All existence derives its intelligibility from the Divine Mind. All human life derives its genesis and end from that for which it strives for union, whether in truth or in idolatry (in the words of G. K. Chesterton, "The man who knocks on the door of a brothel is looking for God"). The sacred and the secular are two divisions of religiosity, for religiosity is encompassing of all contingent being. Even the birds of the air and the lilies of the field exist in a created order for which they were willed into being, that creation might better attain its purpose, that purpose being the glorification of the Creator.

With the eruption of supernatural religion into the world, first with God's covenant with the Israelites and then with the fulfilment of that covenant in Jesus Christ, the distinction arose between the secular and the sacred. That is, the distinction between what God has made to His glory, and what God has redeemed and transfigured, that what He has made might achieve that purpose. Hence, again, both the secular and the sacred are religious. The secular and the sacred are assumed into the Church as two divisions of its existence, namely in what is lay and what is clerical, and together these divisions reflect the sacred humanity and the divine personhood of Jesus Christ. The secular and the sacred accordingly perpetuate the mystery of the Incarnation down the centuries.

"Secularism," then, is simply the name for a kind of onto-logical schizophrenia, in which the secular denies its own essence and repudiates that which comes from without for the achievement of its end. Secularism is a pathology, a fiction, and what it claims as true will never be brought into reality. Secular regimes are thus invariably religious in the most tragic, confused, and chaotic ways. In this volume, I highlight North Korea as an avowedly atheistic state that is nonetheless possessed by its own gods and consequently passionately religious in the worst possible way. It is easy, of course, to point the finger at a despotic land like that, but the so-called secular West is equally religious and equally dishonest about it. We too are religious in a way that profoundly damages the reputation of the word, captured as we are by the basest forms of superstition, idolatry, and appetite for performative ritual and paraliturgy. It only takes a moment of cogitation to think of a host of examples to illustrate what I'm alluding to.

When discussing the phenomenon of secularism, it is now customary to invoke the name of Charles Taylor and his remarkably influential work *The Secular Age*. Whilst there are many merits to that work, and I agree more or less with the diagnosis of the modern condition, I do not believe that Christians need to accommodate themselves to the ailments of "secularism" just as I do not believe they need to accommodate their cognition to the prejudices of ideological frameworks or their conception of human nature to the anthropology of the deracinated, individualist "self." Indeed, I do not believe that Christians should accommodate themselves, or weigh up the feasibility of their own religious commitments, in the light of conditions wrought by any particular error. The role of a Christian in the face of such corruption of reality is to reject it outright and undergo the hard slog of retrieving a pre-modern mind and heart. Felicitous it is, then, that whilst under natural circumstances such a retrieval would be impossible, the circumstances of the Christian layman — who is my primary concern — are not merely natural. The circumstances of the Christian layman are *secular* — that is to say, they are what is natural when transfigured by what is supernatural, which is what the term "secular" meant and ought still to mean.

It is the great fiction of secular*ism* that has led, in fact, to one of Jesus Christ's teachings being probably His most misunderstood teaching: that we should render unto Caesar that which is Caesar's, and unto God that which is God's (Mark 12:17; Matthew 22:21; Luke 20:25). Anyone who reads this passage and infers that Christ is setting up Caesar and the Creator as two equivalent authorities, towards which one has distinct and separate duties, has understood nothing about Christ's ministry and mission. Moreover, Jesus Christ explicitly declares that Pilate — Caesar's representative — would have *no* authority were his authority not participating in the divine authority and power of God (John 19:11). And St. Paul spells it out for the Church that all temporal power is religious in nature (Romans 13:1–7).

It would, it seems, be more appropriate to interpret the Lord's teaching on the duties to Caesar and to God as an example of Jesus Christ laughing at those who would seek to ensnare Him (Psalm 37:12–13). One can only render in justice unto Caesar that which belongs to Caesar when one realises that *all* that belongs to Caesar is held by him as a steward and custodian. For ultimately, and most accurately, *everything* belongs to God, including Caesar himself. Indeed, when St. Peter, the Church's first pope, declared that we must all honour Caesar, the particular holder of that title was then the Christian-persecuting, sodomising lunatic and arsonist Emperor Nero (1 Peter 2:7). In what possible way could or should Christians have honoured such a man? They could honour him as one who, as the Lord declared, received his power from above.

When that enormous empire — that "antichrist," as John Henry Newman called the Roman Empire — was seeking to search out Christians and feed them to lions, St. Peter

was setting up his headquarters *inside* the headquarters of
that great enemy of the Church. Such a decision strikes one
as crossing the line from courageous to foolish, unless the
Christians of the early Church knew that one day even the
Roman Emperors would prostrate themselves with fear and
trembling before the simple carpenter whom their dominion
crucified as a common criminal. In short, the teaching on
rendering to Caesar what is Caesar's and to God what is
God's is what today we would call ironic.

It is part of the twistedness of modernity that whilst
everything our Lord taught is relativised or historicised
into waffle, the one teaching that most obviously expresses
rabbinical humour is taken as the foundation of modern
society-building. The reason for this is simple: the erroneous
but widespread interpretation of our Lord's teaching takes
the temporal domain out of the hands of God. By so doing,
it achieves exactly what modern man wants: to exclude God
from public life. Any Christian who thus endorses a "secularist" social and political settlement has joined his voice
to those of God's enemies.

This corruption of the Lord's teaching entails that God is
no longer the *Ground of being*, but a trinket of our emotional
lives, to be sentimentally enjoyed in the hidden cloisters
of our hearts. Such an inversion of Jesus Christ's teaching
would be amusing were it not blasphemous. Moreover, there
are few teachings of the Lord that have been so consistently
misinterpreted with such considerable and deleterious consequences in practice. For in the modern age, we insist that it
belongs to our civilisation's maturity to exclude God from
public life and mention our duties to Him only with some
embarrassment. The upshot is that our appetite for the
infinite has been transposed onto finite things as we have
replaced the Creator with his creatures. Hence, "modernity"
is not so much a historical epoch but a moral paradigm; it
is the social and political paradigm of idolatry and slavery
to appetite, the overall result of which is a vast mass of
extremely emotionally chaotic and stupid people, ripe for

the looming slave settlement of late, decadent modernity.

Perhaps no nation so successfully yet surreptitiously excluded God from His own creation than the nations of the British Isles. Who knows if the reason for this is the Reformation, or our particular religious war between King Charles I and the coup orchestrated by Parliament and the Roundhead militia, or the Whig ascendency following 1688, or the need for a social cohesion built along lines other than religious ones to achieve the aims of empire? In any case, what the English in particular — and the British in general — realised, was that it was necessary to enter a secularist paradigm, keeping only the "externals" of religiosity for the sake of "dignifying" what was otherwise a work of ongoing secularism. Hence, a deeply ingrained social proclivity emerged of treating any religious feeling that verged on what the English called "enthusiasm" with intense suspicion.

This tendency towards secularisation was not emotionally uncomplicated for the English in particular, for they are at bottom a passionately religious people. For this reason, each time secularism became so dominant that it grew unbearable for the English soul, England experienced some great religious revival. Such happened in the 17th century with the explosion of dissenter sects who then competed for supremacy against the Laudians' Romanising endeavours, in the 18th century with the great spiritual movement that came to be known as "Methodism," and in the 19th century with the Tractarians and their progeny all scattered on both sides of the Tiber. You see, an English religious outburst seems to happen about every hundred years; the next one appears to be a little late, but also not far off.

A religious awakening may be currently bubbling under the surface in deep Albion. Elite powerholders have sought to suppress such a religious awakening by routinely conjoining the nation's religious appetite to petty secularist causes. This tactic has frustrated the religiosity of these Isles, but it has not killed it, and soon it will likely re-emerge as a genuine religious movement. Nonetheless, disdain for religious "enthusiasm" remains a chief characteristic of this unhappy land; regarding how long such a prevailing feature can last, the jury is still out.

The British Establishment's disapproval of public religiosity was exported to every corner of the world, first nascently in the British Empire and then through its fiendish child in American pop culture, now disseminated universally through smart technology and social media. Britain, however, in many respects had its revolution too early — 101 years before the real age of revolution began in 1789 — and hence Britain's revolution wasn't very revolutionary. (This is something Edmund Burke famously observed in the opening quarter of his *Reflections on the Revolution in France*.) And for this reason, Britain's revolution did only half the job. Consequently, quite accidentally, and certainly paradoxically, Britain remains today among the last remnants of Christendom.

Britain, constitutionally and socially, has one foot in the old Christian order of our civilisation and one foot in the revolutionism of modernity. In these isles you will find an ancient stone church in every village. Church towers and spires punctuate the landscape. The land is governed together by MPs (once called "knights of the shires") and an upper chamber of lords spiritual and temporal, over which sits a sacral monarch, under whose diadem sacred chrism is drawn. But since the Stuarts, the sacral monarchy's power has been usurped and held by those who were its servants and emissaries. The lords are now an oligarchical cabal of progressives who disdain the remaining hereditary peers among them. The established Church has little to do with the Christian religion, and its empty buildings now find new uses as cafes and bingo halls. To live in modern Britain is to live in the shadow of a great yet destroyed civilisation, among a population stumbling in the dark with little knowledge of how it came to be or where it is going.

The character of Britain, which makes it a land ever divided against itself, accounts for the idiosyncratic nature of its species of "conservatism." The British are stuck firmly in the revolutionary paradigm. They are stuck by necessity. For, ever since the Whig ascendency, which entailed the final quashing of the formal tie with Christendom in these isles, the challenge facing powerholders has been that of how to uproot — so as to turn into mere instruments of use — a population that so instinctively and committedly attaches itself to places and traditions. The enclosure operations from the 17th to the 19th centuries, enshrined in law by oligarchical parliamentarians, were the most overtly brutish examples of such manoeuvres of deracination. There have been many others over the centuries, though, often far more tacit and seductive.

This pattern can be seen in the contributions of Richard Curtis to British film and television. His productions offer an image of middle-class England where everyone is wealthy and largely carefree, and in this way he is the perfect British *regime producer*. Curtis shows his fellow countrymen that, whatever happens, "there'll always be England," as the old song goes. But he fills such visions of England, an England that hasn't been observable in reality for decades, with stories of loose relations, homosexuality, and family breakdown repackaged as "truth to self." One interesting example was his television show *The Vicar of Dibley*, hugely popular throughout the 1990s, in which a fat female vicar slowly conforms a traditional rural English village to the maxims of revolutionary modernity, whilst engaging in casual sexual relations and encouraging religious indifference among her parishioners. She does this, however, without dramatically upsetting the aesthetics of the village. The message is clear: *do not fear getting with the programme, we won't tamper with things too much — all will turn out okay, you'll see.* Hence, the perfect balance is struck between aggressive progressivism and superficial conservatism, which is just the right balance to successfully dupe the typical Brit whilst avoiding flustering him. In the last episode ever made, the fat vicaress walks into the middle of the village green and pins up a Black Lives Matter poster, "takes the knee," and holds her fist in the air in support of what is in fact a racist, communist organisation responsible for sacking whole cities on both sides of the Atlantic. Such a gesture would have been impossible at the beginning of the series, but by the end, the viewership was sufficiently sedated and desensitised by the whole operation.

That is but one example taken from low, popular culture (or anti-culture), and perhaps as an example it is a frivolous one. Much graver examples, however, can be highlighted which reveal the very same pattern. When David Cameron declared in 2011, "I don't support gay marriage in spite of being a Conservative; I support gay marriage *because* I'm a Conservative," he was following the time-tested methodology of English revolutionary "conservatism." Had a member of the Labour Party or even the Liberal Democrats attempted such an aggressive operation of social engineering, that so evidently undermines the natural family (the very bedrock and foundation of civil society), many would have insisted that Britain was being subjected to a social experiment for ideological purposes. But as this astonishingly revolutionary act was packaged as a conservative feat, Brits continued to sip their tea and feel that all was safe and steady.

The example of the Conservative Party's redefinition of marriage with its "Marriage (Same Sex Couples) Act 2013" and that of the fictitious Vicar of Dibley are worth bringing together, because they highlight the two main institutions of revolution in the United Kingdom. Since the great apostasy of these isles following Henry VIII's libidinous and mur-derous fit, two prevailing institutions were established: the Church of England and the Conservative Party. These two institutions always shared a certain kinship that was known to all, and they ever benefited from each other's rapaciousness and craving for power.[1] The role of the Church of England down the centuries has largely been that of consolidating the

---

[1]  For example, H.J. Massingham comments on the considerable profits gained by the Anglican clergy from the continual Enclosure Acts, which, as he puts it, "destroyed our peasantry." See *The Tree of Life* (New York: Angelico Press, 2024; originally published in 1943), 132.

nation's apostasy whilst ever maintaining among the populace some sense that they still have the Christian religion. Correspondingly, the role of the Conservative Party has been that of advancing the transition into secular modernity without ever letting the populace feel that they're in the throes of a revolution. These correlated roles have not, I think, arisen from an intended conspiracy of some cabal of clerics and policymakers against the people — not at all times, anyway. Here, I think, we are in the realm of "egregores."[2]

The virtues of both institutions and many of the individuals who have belonged to them ought not to be disregarded. Our civilisation would be poorer were it not for the conserving of many of the nation's traditions by the Church of England — especially its glorious choral tradition — and the perpetuation of old Toryism, at least for a time, in the Conservative Party.[3] Nonetheless, it is on account of these two leading institutions that dominated the social life of Britain for centuries that the population was able successfully to sleepwalk into atheism, materialism, individualism, and ultimately nihilism. The observable collapse of the Church of England and the Conservative Party, which appears to be

---

[2] The notion entailed by the term 'egregore' is that it is possible for ideas to take on a certain existence of their own, leading or governing those committed to them. It is a term drawn from Western esotericism and can be useful in considering human psychology as it is when fettered by ideology. Maistre seems to have something comparable to 'egregore' in mind when he writes: "[T]he French Revolution leads men more than men lead it.... The very rascals who appear to lead the Revolution are involved as simple instruments." Joseph de Maistre, *Considerations on France*, edited by Richard A. Lebrun (Cambridge: Cambridge University Press, 1994), 5.

[3] I define Toryism elsewhere in the following way: "Toryism is the British, or Anglo, variety of traditional conservatism. Toryism tends to defend inherited institutions and hierarchies of society and State as well as civil liberties and responsibilities. Strongly opposed to liberalism and radicalism, Toryism emphasises organicism, received custom, and has always been associated with defence of Church establishment, tending towards 'high church' or 'ritualist' forms of belief and practice." *Conservatism and Grace: The Conservative Case for Religion by Establishment* (London: Routledge, 2023), 53, n. 23.

accelerating, is likely occurring because their sheer success has rendered them obsolete.[4]

In these isles, there has ever been a mythology of "English liberties," even as we have become the most watched population on earth outside China with new surveillance technologies, which now even include AI-operated face-recognition software. Still, that myth of old inherited liberties from our Anglo-Saxon forebears lives on in the back of our minds. And for the reason of this myth — which is really no myth at all, but a curse — never would the English have accepted the COVID restrictions and the coercion to take experimental "vaccines," had such pressure not come from a Conservative government. But because such pressure came from the Conservatives, the COVID panic was not deemed by Brits to be what in fact it was, namely a huge power-grabbing operation by transnational, centralising powers, which utilised psychological terror tactics to effect compliance. The deep, deep conservatism of the British Isles' inhabitants means, at bottom, that the revolutionary endeavours of its oligarchs will not be accepted unless they are presented as conservative endeavours. The procedurally established oligarchs are pleased to oblige in repackaging their operations as conservative for the sake of securing acquiescence. *This* is the utter perniciousness of the Anglo-conservative paradigm. Unfortunately, this paradigm has become the dominant model of democratic revolutionism since World War II.

*Modern* globalist progressivism is largely an admixture of that bourgeois liberalism of the Anglo world and the much

---

[4] To my ongoing amazement, the sacral and organic culture of this Sceptred Isle somehow lives on, despite the fact that it suffers from the relentless hostile attention of powerholders, who continuously seek to legislate and tax it out of existence, presumably hoping finally to reduce the population to politically *useful* atomic units of production and consumption. Nevertheless, astonishingly, there's still an old pub in almost every village serving real ale, countryside sports and their associated traditions endure, county shows appear up and down the land during the clement months, and old folk songs are still learned and performed. My hope is that I do not belong to the last generation to enjoy these gifts of our ancestors.

more violent progressivism of the land over the Channel, France, which sought to impose the most aggressive rationalism across the world by means of war in the 18th and 19th centuries. France did as a corporate person what individual progressives do throughout the course of their lives, namely inflict on the rest of the world their unresolved infelicities, or at least their inability to reconcile themselves to the fact that unhappiness and suffering are the normal conditions of human existence. For this reason, in this book, I give some attention to France. After all, Edmund Burke, whilst railing against the developments across the Channel that he observed in his own lifetime, was keen also to point out the indebtedness of European, Christian civilisation to France. He addresses the French nation thus:

> It is not clear, whether in England we learned those grand and decorous principles, and manners, of which considerable traces yet remain, from you, or whether you took them from us. But to you, I think, we trace them best. You seem to me to be — *gentis incunabula nostrae.* France has always more or less influenced manners in England; and when your fountain is choked up and polluted, the stream will not run long, or not run clear with us, or perhaps with any nation. This gives all Europe, in my opinion, but too close and connected a concern in what is done in France.[5]

I entirely agree with Burke. France has always held, and always will hold, a special place in our civilisation, and France's apostasy and downfall will continue to have consequences for all nations that even now are not yet fully known.

Burke understood our civilisation and he offered a pragmatic and prudence-driven approach to its conservation. The unfortunate consequence of the adoption of his approach has been the concession by conservatives of ever more moral and social territory to the onslaught of progressivism. Accordingly,

---

[5] Edmund Burke, *Reflections on the Revolution in France* (London: Penguin Books, 1986), 174–175.

as noted, much "conservatism" in our own time is little more than a species of liberalism. Joseph de Maistre, on the other hand, offered an entire religious metaphysics and meta-historiography in his attack on modernity and revolutionism, but he provided no conceptual mechanism to prevent his contribution from degenerating into another ideological competitor in the modern arena of "systems." Without being tempered by questions of prudence, his approach would seek to conform the world to a set of *a priori* moral and doctrinal commitments. Part of the case I advanced in my doctoral research, which was eventually developed and published as a Routledge monograph in 2023 under the title of *Conservatism and Grace*, was that any authentic, future conservatism in defence of our received civilisation — or what's left of it — would need something like a creative synthesis of Maistrean scrutiny and Burkean practice. It is out of such a view of conservatism, or what I prefer to call "traditionalism," that the chapters in this book have unfolded.

This synthesis of Maistreanism and Burkeanism raises the ever-pressing question of how the eternal and the temporal, the celestial and the terrestrial, meet each other in our individual and shared experience. And thus, we return to the title of this book. For the human experience is one across time, of ages after ages, epochs after epochs, in which we must decide whether freedom comes from inducting ourselves into our civilisation or emancipating ourselves from it. Modernity has indubitably opted for the latter viewpoint, and consequently we have found ourselves not free — as we had hoped — but uprooted, confused, purposeless, and traumatised.

The Greek word "aiōnes," what in English we term "ages," can entail temporal reality, either as *time* or spatial existence, meaning something like *world* or *universe*; but it can also mean *all* existence inclusive of both heavenly and earthly reality. In turn, the Latin phrase *In Saecula Saeculorum*, taken from the Greek εἰς τοὺς αἰῶνας τῶν αἰώνων, does not only evoke in the mind connotations of the secular-sacred distinction and relation, with which this Introduction began, but the age-ageless distinction and relation. And it is reconciling *our* age, before it is too late, with the Ages of Ages — expressing not only the idea of eternity but its intimations in our finite world — which is the primary imperative of the political traditionalist, a task that has never been more daunting at any other time in history.

Reconciling the temporal with the perennial, which is a decent summary of the mission or apostolate of the lay person, is not, however, merely an intellectual task. The lay person is not principally interested in a mere philosophical, speculative enterprise, much less a sophistical game of conceptual conjoinings. The lay person, when his identity is brought to fruition, is chiefly a person of practical and prudential genius. His purpose is to capture not only moral, intellectual, and cultural regions of the devil's principality, but literal earthly regions, and place all that can be redeemed under the Kingship of Jesus Christ. He does this in the most overt way by assuming the natural constitutions of his polities into the divine constitution of Christ's Mystical Body, the Church, thereby realising the discipleship of nations (Matthew 28:19). And he does this in the most quotidian but no less important way by giving his home, his business, and his leisure to Jesus Christ. Thus, I end this book with some more practical meditations on the diabolical seductiveness of pop culture, and the need for the baptised, together, to revitalise authentic culture, take aesthetics seriously, and spend time with one another as families and friends. These final chapters may seem flippant, but they certainly are not.

# PART I
# FOR THE LOVE
# OF HOME

# THE HUMAN PERSON
# IS ENDANGERED

I BELIEVE THE HUMAN PERSON IS ENDAN-
gered. Let me explain what I mean by that. Three centuries ago, a debate was introduced into the public arena
by Jean-Jacques Rousseau. This debate—which remains very
much alive—centres on whether the "authentic individual"
exists prior to his life in society, or rather emerges *out* of
his life in society. Downstream from this debate are two
claims that remain at the heart of the progressive/conser-
vative dichotomy.

For the progressive, one ought to enjoy the advantages
of society whilst always emancipating himself from society,
to maintain his "authentic self." Society is always a threat
to his "authentic self," and hence, necessarily, in some way
tyrannical—of a patriarchal kind or otherwise—and it must
ever be purified through ongoing revolution. In turn, the
progressive will always favour the atomised and *alienated*
individual over the accountable and *communally bound* individual who is formed by local and national loyalties.

For traditional conservatives, attacks on the settled or
national way of life do not emancipate individuals from a
disguised captivity. Rather, they threaten the very foundation
of social relations within which emerges the human *person*—
by which I mean the unique, irreplaceable individual who
takes possession of his life and governs himself, so as to be
in right relation with others. Society isn't some looming,
*external* force: society is us, and we are society.

Unique, irreplaceable individuals—that is to say, *persons*—result from their civilisation. Persons don't opt into
their communities by some primordial contract. (Indeed,

"nation" has the same etymology as the word "natal" — the nation is that from which we are born into the world.) Human beings actualise their *personhood* precisely by being inducted into the communities from which they have come, with their histories, cultures, laws, and customs. Via this process, people cease to be slaves to ignorance and appetite, and they discover their *personal* freedom.

*This* is the paradoxical truth of traditional conservatives: such people hold that it is by being inducted into our received, shared civilisation that our uniqueness as individual persons unfolds. Accordingly — and perhaps counterintuitively for the modern mind — *tradition* and *freedom* are correlated principles.

The process of liberal atomisation and deracination has made very difficult the sort of civilisational induction that is necessary for personal actuation. This means that we may be seeing a process by which — as the German philosopher Robert Spaemann suggested — persons may vanish altogether.[1]

Already, those in the vanguard of our progressive culture are increasingly like clones of one another. They claim to have realised their supposed uniqueness and authenticity while simultaneously embracing a narrow groupthink, parroting the same narratives, and even sporting the same blue hair. Emancipated from their received civilisation, these presocietal "authentic selves" turn out to be interchangeable with all other such selves.

Human personhood is a phenomenon poised in the dynamism of human sociality. Persons emerge out of community, and communities are very thin within the paradigm of liberal-progressive individualism.

*Real* communities are moral units, with shared notions of purpose and meaning by which their members may live together. For this reason, any given society, at root, is religious; for all societies, inasmuch as they are societies, are bound by some shared set of beliefs and practices pertaining

---

[1]  See Robert Spaemann, *Persons: The Difference between 'Someone' and 'Something'* (Oxford: Oxford University Press, 2017), 18.

to the most fundamental questions about our purpose, dignity, and destiny as a human community.

What does such a claim mean in the context of my own country? In England, we have a national religion with a Church by law established and enshrined in our constitution, a glorious affirmation of which we saw not long ago during the King's coronation. This established religion, however, is not the one we actually practise.

190 years have passed since the Reverend John Keble ascended Oxford's university pulpit and declared that the nation had committed apostasy, a sermon that launched the Tractarian Movement, which in turn revitalised Toryism, inspiring the Young Englanders who gave us Benjamin Disraeli.[2] But that revival didn't last, and as John Henry Newman wrote, "Toryism came to pieces and went the way of all flesh."[3] In any case, what I think someone like Keble, or Disraeli, or Newman, could never have envisaged was the nation's replacement of Christianity with a new religion altogether.

In recent years, there has been a lot of talk about the social phenomenon of "woke." Among conservative-minded people, the instinctive response in the face of "woke" is to criticise it and ridicule it as both hysterical and censorious. But I remain unconvinced that we have diagnosed "woke" properly. We should see it for what it is, namely an expression of a very deep and noble religious need, a need that has been neglected and mistreated in contemporary British society and everywhere secularism has become the dominant social and political paradigm.

In essence, "woke" simply treats questions of ethnic identity, historical culpability, systemic oppression, and long-standing injustice — and hence questions of shared meaning, purpose, and destiny — as questions that are both public and

---

[2] John Keble, 'National Apostasy', preached on the 14th of July 1833 at St. Mary's, Oxford, https://anglicanhistory.org/keble/keble1.html

[3] John Henry Newman, *A Letter Addressed to the Duke of Norfolk* ([n.p.] Aeterna Press, 2015), 54.

relevant, and question that take priority over those of the economy and "individual rights." In that regards, "woke," as a movement, is entirely correct in its assumptions; its great fault has been its adherents' refusal to accept answers to those questions that differ from those to which their own ideological impulses would lead them, and their craving to destroy their opponents rather than debate with them.

The zeal observed among today's "woke" progressives marks a deeply religious attempt to provide a rapidly fragmenting community with a sense of common purpose. Unfortunately, it is failing to do so. I join the company of numerous commentators who have highlighted the religious character of our progressivist culture: it has its own theology; its moral decrees; its sacrificial victims; its proselytizers; a highly effective inquisition; an exegetical methodology for interpreting history; an index of forbidden books; its iconography — especially the "selfie," that frozen avatar of the disembodied "authentic self"; it has its saints and martyrs; its doctrine of healthcare and safety as the topmost ethical values; its idolatry of technologies as the angelic mediators that will bring about a new heaven and a new earth; and it promotes the LGBTQ+ movement as the highest religious expression, with its public processions, flags and banners, and a liturgical year complete with holy days and months of festivities. And this religion sees the State as a "mortal god" — to use the words of Thomas Hobbes — that will bestow the infinite capital-P "Progress" for which we beg. And everyone must join in the devotions of this public religion that promises not to redeem our human nature, but rather our de-natured "authentic selves" by vanquishing human nature altogether, and those who are insufficiently enthusiastic are judged heretics and are driven from polite society.

The problem is that whilst this counterfeit religion purports to unify us in pursuit of an egalitarian utopia of infinite progress, it simultaneously atomises us in pursuit of the pre-societal "authentic self" — the *only* self that can ever be truly equal to all other selves. Thus, whilst purporting to offer a loose conception of the good around which it can gather society, it concurrently divides us all in the paradigm of isolation and social repudiation.

And what is the upshot? Whilst communication has never been so accessible and belief in social activism never so widespread, statistically Britons, for example, haven't before felt so insulated and so alienated; currently the leading cause of death among teenagers and adults up to the age of 34 is suicide. My country is deeply, deeply unwell, and it is not alone in its maladies.

As the 18th century conservative Joseph de Maistre observed, an atomised people is a miserable and vulnerable people who will be forced to grovel before a divinised, all-encompassing administrative juggernaut.[4] What someone like Maistre could never have imagined was the emergence of a massive information and surveillance industry, working as one mechanism across much of the globe, manipulating almost every facet of life through a sort of technological omnipresence. This Leviathan has now encroached on every aspect of private association and civil society, deeming itself the providential lord of history. And this technologically driven globalism is now threatening to eliminate the human person by defeating his nature altogether via the vastly funded sorcery of transhumanism. It seems we are witnessing, to put things back into Maistre's idiom, the capture of our world by the forces of Satan's principality.[5]

The self-identification of global Leviathan as providential lord of history cast off all its concealments during the Covid hysteria from 2020–2023, for which there has not been a proper reckoning. In the UK, under a Tory government,

---

[4]  See my extended analysis of Maistre's anti-modern and counter-revolutionary politics in *Conservatism and Grace*, 100–176, 235–275.

[5]  See Joseph de Maistre, *The Pope: Considered in His Relations with the Church, Temporal Sovereignties, Separated Churches, and the Cause of Civilization*, translated by Aeneas McDonell Dawson (London: C. Dolman, 1850), xxiii.

people were confined to their homes, with many plunged
into crushing debt; the police morphed into roaming thugs;
panic was deliberately fostered; experimental drugs were
imposed with threats of unemployment if people didn't
acquiesce, with many now suffering from vaccine-injuries
remaining largely ignored by their government; and senior
Tory ministers co-opted the public into a surveillance system
by asking them to spy on their neighbours. This sort of
autocracy was duplicated across the world.

Such a regime is what you should expect, as persons as
we know them vanish from our world and are replaced with
human cogs in a colossal global machine. This is why, with
every fibre of his being, Edmund Burke condemned what he
called "atheism by establishment", which would lend itself to
the politics of "a mischievous and ignoble oligarchy with a
purely geometrical and arithmetical" conception of society.[6]

The challenge that Burke faced at the dawn of our secular
age hasn't changed: he was opposing an atheistic, imperial
technocracy in embryonic form; *we* are facing it in maturity.
The choices remain: nihilism or God — or put differently,
idolatry and captivity masquerading as pleasure and safety,
*or* the genuine freedom, meaning, and purpose that comes
from acknowledging the spiritual dimension of who we
are. Whether human personhood vanishes altogether will
depend on how we choose.

Allow me to summarise. Either persons precede society
as so-called "authentic selves," merely opting into society
for its advantages; *or* persons emerge out of society, that
is, a meaning-driven community of people who belong
together, animated by a sense of transcendent purpose. In
short, between nihilism and the divine there is no medium.
Either way, however, as Disraeli famously observed, man will

---

[6] Edmund Burke, 'Letters on a Regicide Peace' in *The Works of the Rt.
Hon. Edmund Burke* (London: Henry G. Bohn, 1854), vol. 13, 170–171;
*Reflections on the Revolution in France* (London: Penguin Books, 1986),
228, 144.

worship *something*.[7] The question is, then: what cultus, and by extension what culture, do we want to have? One that unites us in a common moral project by which we emerge together as persons, or something else?

In the UK, I believe it's time to retrieve a genuine, theocentric conservatism, which can offer a spiritual and moral vision of the human person. If conservatism in the UK and beyond continues to be nothing other than diluted a version of its more progressive competitors, conservatism won't only lose its place in the public arena altogether but it will entirely deserve to do so. At present, in the UK and among all the heirs to the great Western tradition, there is a widespread hunger for a serious spiritual and moral account of who we are and our common purpose. This hunger will be ignored by us at our peril.

---

[7] "Man is made to adore and to obey; but if you will not command him, if you give him nothing to worship, he will fashion his own divinities, and find a chieftain in his own passions." Benjamin Disraeli, *Coningsby: Or, The New Generation* (London: H. Colburn, 1844), 223.

# 2

# THE NEED FOR NOSTALGIA

THE MEANING OF "CONSERVATISM" has been incrementally changed since conservative movements emerged in the early Enlightenment era to defend the old European political and religious order, a phenomenon that received the name of "conservatism" from François-René de Chateaubriand's *Le Conservateur*, his anti-revolutionary journal in the early-19th century. The meaning of the term was dramatically changed in the UK in the 19th century, largely on account of Prime Minister Robert Peel and his creation of a Tory-Whig hybrid party in the 1830s. It was further corrupted in the 20th century, especially by the neoliberal movement of the Thatcher-Reagan alliance which called itself "conservative" towards the tail end of the Cold War. What the word "conservative" actually means in the political and social context, then, can be a somewhat contentious issue.

The utility of the word "conservative" is unclear to me. But I believe that *if* we are going to keep using the word, it is imperative to recover it in such a way that it denotes what it was always meant to denote. Indeed, happily, there are still enough people out there for whom "conservative" *does* denote the counter-revolutionary, historically based cause for establishmentarian Christianity. That is to say, for a struggling remnant, "conservative" still means what it did for those who opposed the age of revolution at its inception. In the face of revolutionary secularism, social atheism, materialism, amorality, and rationalistic *tabula rasa* political ideology, conservatives wanted to protect the Christian religion enshrined in the law of those political orders that providentially and organically emerged down the centuries. Without qualification, this is what *I* mean by conservatism.

Consequently, I hold that "conservatism" applied to groups outside historically Christian lands is, and always has been, an equivocation — perhaps a legitimate one, but an equivocation all the same.

## CHRISTENDOM OR LIBERALISM

The movement and loyalties of old Toryism — the traditional British species of conservatism — began during the reign of the Stuarts as a response to the Protestant dissenters. Toryism was primarily based on the conviction that the Church ought to be public and enshrined in law, rather than reduced to the sentiments of the cloistered conscience of each individual. This is a point well-developed in a sophisticated historical analysis by James J. Sack in his 1993 book *From Jacobite to Conservative*, whose central thesis is that Toryism as a distinct social tradition orbited a Christian, establishmentarian political cause.[1]

Back in the mid-17th century, the Protestant dissenter groups — who considered the established Church in England to be what they called "Romish" — banded together, utilising Parliament to establish a military coup d'état, to fight and ultimately behead the martyr-king Charles I. Soon after committing their monstrous act of regicide, they established under their leader Oliver Cromwell the first absolutist, totalitarian dictatorship that the Christian world had ever seen — calling this new regime the "Liberty of Conscience."

Despite the manifest illiberalism of the dissenters, the old Tories intuited that subordinating religion to private conviction after the dissenter fashion, and thereby relegating it from the public form of the state to the subjective sentiments of the private conscience, would lead to the kind of relativism which would fragment society into a crowd of atomic strangers, as we have witnessed under the global regime of liberalism. This is a point that was well argued by St. John Henry Newman in his "Biglietto Speech," delivered in 1879 on becoming a

---

[1] *From Jacobite to Conservative: Reaction and Orthodoxy in Britain, 1760–1832* (Cambridge: Cambridge University Press, 1993).

cardinal of the Catholic Church, wherein he offered an apo-
logia for the English conception of establishmentarian Christianity, and condemned the Protestant dissenter tradition as
the true enemy of Christendom. Liberalism and revolution
in religion, Newman argued, was inherently bound up with
liberalism and revolution in politics.[2]

In that speech, Newman was in fact echoing the nation's
first Poet Laureate, John Dryden, who two centuries earlier,
in his poem *The Hind and the Panther* — written soon after
Dryden's conversion to Catholicism — called for an alliance
of Catholics and High Anglicans against the dissenters
whom he feared would undo any shared conception of a
visible Church. That is, he called for unity among those who
believed in established Christianity, composed of clerical and
lay orders, against those who believed in, as Dryden put it in
his prologue to the poem, "faith according to conscience."[3]
The entire Tory tradition, until the word was appropriated
by its enemies, held that there were two options available:
Christendom or liberalism.

The Tories historically resembled conservative movements
in other countries, especially the French royalists, the Spanish
Carlists, and the Habsburg loyalists of the old Imperial lands
of *Mitteleuropa*. In each nation that has faced the forces of
modernity — egalitarianism, subjectivist relativism, materialism, positivism, atheism — conservative movements have
risen based on the notion that man is inherently religious
and his religiosity cannot be extinguished, that religion is
public, and that true religion is the proper form of the state,
by which the nation, whose political realisation *is* the state,
may in turn be discipled.

What distinguishes true conservatism as I understand it
from the neoliberalism that has adopted the name of "conservatism" in the late modern age, is that the latter has held

---

[2] See John Henry Newman, '*Biglietto* Speech', https://www.newman-
reader.org/works/addresses/file2.html
[3] See John Dryden, 'The Hind and the Panther' in *Selected Poems*
(London: Penguin Classics, 2001), 222.

as true the very lie of the dissenters which conservatism arose in the early Enlightenment era to oppose. That is, the view that religion is private and only the regulation of trade and property — what is increasingly termed "growth" — is of legitimate public concern. Thus, what we now call "conservatism" is the very "atheism by establishment" that the crypto-Tory Edmund Burke condemned by name as the antithesis of all he stood for. The epitome of such phoney conservatism is the UK Conservative Party, which now largely exists to prevent any genuine conservative revival in the isles I call my home.

## INTEGRALISM AND THE ABSTRACT

As I understand it, what distinguishes true conservatism from the movement that goes by the name of "integralism," is that conservatism does not reduce the relationship of Church and State merely to the acknowledgement of some abstract principle — for example, that all legislation be first subordinated to the requirements of the present curia and its interpretation of the faith.[4] Rather, conservatives take an historical view, deeming establishmentarian Christianity to denote nothing other than the historical permeation and transformation of nature by grace, the *polis* belonging as it does to human nature.

It is common today to see Christianity primarily as a set of propositions requiring assent rather than as the existential transformation of nature by grace. This is largely due to the spell of rationalism which causes the mind to privilege the abstract over the concrete, the theoretical over the historical, the absolute over the conditional, the principled over the practised, and the mechanistic over the organic.

Due to the rationalism prevalent in our age, we are far more comfortable with abstract principles than we are with stories. But God tells stories. And when the Eternal Word, having

---

[4] For a helpful analysis of the political theology movement known as 'integralism' and the claims of some of its leading proponents, see Charlie Camosy, *What is integralism, anyway?*, https://www.pillarcatholic.com/p/what-is-integralism-anyway

assumed our nature from the Blessed Virgin, was personally present among us in the person of Jesus Christ, he did not deliver lists of theological formulae, but instead he told stories. What above all interests conservatives is the stories of their nations and the way in which God has existentially made Himself present among those nations. Conservatives have a far higher regard for concrete history than Platonic speculations.

Thus, it is not primarily *principle* that is of concern to conservatives, but *narrative*. God reveals Himself through the story of a nation — that of the Israelites — to which He gives a territory. The mission of His incarnation reaches out into the world through the Great Commission to make disciples of all *nations*. And it is specifically the *nations* which have been redeemed that come at the eschaton to worship the Lamb enthroned, gathering in the New Jerusalem, as chapter 22 of the Book of the Apocalypse tells us. God's revelation is the story of His assumption of political units into His divine life, and that acknowledgement is at the heart of establishmentarianism, which has itself always been the core cause of *true* conservatives.

Whilst I am in agreement with the Catholic integralists that life will return to our dying nations only by rekindling fidelity to Jesus Christ, I do not believe that it is by commitment to a principle that our nations will return to Him. And if it were by commitment to a principle then such a return would be ruinous to itself for it would be driven by a force that is worryingly ideological, and therefore alien to the way God makes Himself known to us down the ages. I am sceptical of any kind of manual or set of formulae for spiritual transformation, because I do not believe that is how divine grace operates. As I see it, the rebuilding of Christendom, if it happens, won't be like repairing a motorcar, but repairing a marriage.

## SHARED AFFECTIONS

If we ever recover from the curse of modernity, it will be by affection for our countrymen, our institutions, our shared history, that by such affection we may come to love again the providential God who has been the source of all our comforts as well as our strength in tribulations, whether we knew it at the time or not. Put differently, recovery will largely rely on the nostalgic impulse. For this reason, conservatives have typically been concerned with art, architecture, and every aspect of high and low cultural renewal — against the escalating encroachment of pop culture and other forms of uglification — because they think that, in Burke's words, "to love our country, our country must be lovely."[5]

The regeneration of the mind — of our *principles*, if you like — is downstream from the regeneration of our experience. And it is the experience of shared affection, far more than any abstract principle, that drives the health of nations. If you were to ask me by what rational principle I love my mother, I could only tell you that I deem the question strange, and any reasons that I gave would be post hoc in any case, and not in reality what has always driven my filial piety. All true love, and hence all true health, is like that, including the love of one's country and love of the God who has sought to draw one's country into the life of discipleship.

The classical liberalism or neoliberalism of today's so-called "conservatives" is morally and ideologically bankrupt, and in any case, it is disappearing in what is being widely referred to as our emerging "meaning-based public discourse," which is rapidly framing the debate about our future on both the Left and the Right. On the other hand, the integralism of post-liberal Catholics risks reducing to an abstractionist exercise what is known by experience and cultural induction, thereby perpetuating the age of ideological squabbles which they ought to be repudiating in entirety. Apart from the traditionalist conservatism to which I have pointed in brief, I see no way out of the age of ideology, which has been so destructive since its beginning.

Of course, I accept that Catholic integralism is a broad allegiance, and indeed I might unknowingly belong to it. But

---

[5] Burke, *Reflections*, 172.

having spent much time studying the works of integralism's advocates — and being greatly enriched by such study, I hasten to add — I note distinct emphases emerge, dividing traditional conservatives like me from integralists, who nonetheless in many respects remain my allies. In general, I have suggested that this division emerges from the historically rooted approach of the conservatives as decidedly different to what I deem the overly abstractionist approach of the growing integralist movement. Put simply, whilst I believe true conservatives can offer an escape route out of the age of ideology, integralists not only risk perpetuating the age of ideology but worse, reducing true religion to but one competing ideology among others in the modernist arena of bickering rationalisms.

# 3

# THE MODERN STATE
# WILL BECOME VERY RELIGIOUS

T HE ENSUING CASE PRESUPPOSES SEV-
eral assumptions, with which one may or may not
agree, but it is necessary to declare them from the
outset for the sake of clarity. I take it as a given that human
nature exists. We are not self-creating beings, nor can we
change our nature. We can warp our nature, mutilate it, and
depart from its laws in innumerable ways that as a civilisation
we are currently exploring with great dedication—but that
is to do violence to our nature, not to change it.

Such a view entails that there is indeed a law of human
nature, with which we can seek to align our lives in our
pursuit of flourishing—or indeed by our own volition we
can depart from that law. The ways by which we may align
ourselves with that law are diverse and dynamic, but such
dynamism presupposes the acknowledgement of such a law.
I further take it as a given that political life—by which I
mean the moral or practical ordering of our lives in community, and its regulation through leadership and positive law-
making—is proper to human nature. As individual persons,
we emerge out of, and naturally maintain, corporate persons.

Such communally reliant flourishing is not accidental
to the kind of things we are, but rather it is proper to
our nature. Humans are not found to be solitary, non-
political animals anywhere on earth, nor have they ever
been such. All philosophies that begin from the assumption that human beings are by nature solitary, and merely
opt into synthetic communities with accidental forms for
some prior, rationally apprehended reason, are flawed in
their principal premise.

Finally, I take it as a given that we are by nature question-asking and meaning-seeking beings, and hence, we are religious by nature. We ask questions about our origin, our purpose, and our ultimate destiny, and we come up with workable answers to those questions. More importantly, we develop art, mythology, and ritual by which we both seek to embody our quest for meaning and seek some personal encounter with the God or the gods who form the object of our devotions. Religion is baked into our nature.

Thus, because human beings are both political and religious by nature, there has never been such a thing as a secular society. Societies have always been religious. The moment society was declared secular in the 18th century by the French *philosophes* and their political activists, that society immediately erupted in a religious frenzy of sacrifice, paraliturgical activity, and the deification of the State as a new providential deity, with all the ritualistic expressions proper to religion subordinated to such anti-religious religiosity.

Given that religion is natural to mankind, and political government is the highest natural authority that exists over mankind — that is, mankind instantiated in his communities, nations, and empires, etc. — the proper authority over the religious life of any given natural community is its government. This fact has always been recognised. The Roman Emperor was arbiter over which were the public gods and which were the hearth gods, and eventually he even placed himself among the former. The Athenian statesmen were the protectors of religious life in their *polis*, and they lawfully executed Socrates for corrupting such religiosity among the young. The barbarian warlords of the north appointed their sacrificial priests and druids just as they appointed their lesser chieftains.

Why, then, is it so alien to us to think of political leaders as the apposite authorities over the religious beliefs and practices of the citizenry? The answer is simple: we are all stumbling about in the shadow of Christendom, and simultaneously we are attempting to run on its fumes.

Political leaders, as the highest authorities in any natural society, are the proper authorities over the religion of their people, which is always some manifestation of natural religion. But our civilisation has historically held that this is the age of Jesus Christ, and consequently *super*natural religion has entered the world. Christians claim that their religion does not have its origin in the natural religious impulse of human nature, but has come into the world from without, and in doing so has assumed into itself that natural religious impulse, has transformed it, and superseded it.

In short, Christians claim that their religion is *not* a natural religion, but a supernatural one. Thus, they claim it requires an institution of purely supernatural origin to be both its interpreter and promulgator, namely the Christian priestly hierarchy. Political leaders, whose role is rooted in the requirements of human nature, are simply not competent to be the highest authorities over this supernatural religion. Thus, in a Christendom model, we have two authoritative institutions on earth, one of natural origin, customarily called the State, and one of supernatural origin, customarily called the Church.

The terminology of Church and State, however, is deeply misleading. States, once they are Christian political communities, are no longer deemed by Christians to be merely natural communities. They are supernaturalised natural communities by virtue of the baptism of their members and the recognition of Christianity by their existent political and legal organs. Thus, in a Christendom model, what we customarily call "Church and State" are more accurately called the spiritual and temporal divisions of the one supernatural community of Christians called the Church. The monarch or prime minister or president of a Christian nation, then, is as much a leader in the Church as any bishop, except as a layman he is ordinarily competent in the temporal matters of that supernatural community, and only extra-ordinarily competent in spiritual and doctrinal matters — whereas this is the reverse for a bishop.

If the Church's kerygmatic enterprise withdraws from the public arena, or it is excluded from that arena by a political movement of apostasy, this has several harmful effects from a Christian perspective. First, the Church atrophies, as it cannot fulfil its own mission, and it increasingly attempts to justify its own existence by presenting itself as a club committed only to temporal concerns, within the jurisdiction of an increasingly anti-religious State. Second, this situation leads to a kind of moral schizophrenia among the baptised — especially baptised statesmen — who are expected to be Christians at home and secularists at work. Third, such an arrangement does not lead to what is widely claimed — namely a religiously neutral public arena.

Some think that if the State remains intentionally neutral with regard to religion, such political indifferentism towards religion will leave the religious life of believers to flourish undisturbed by State interference. On this model, the role of the State is not to protect or promote any one religion in particular, or religious belief in general, but only to protect *religious liberty*. The State would only interfere in the practices of private religious associations if those practices conflicted with State law, such as the ceremonial use of an illegal drug, for example. As John Locke put it, in his *Letter Concerning Toleration*, "these things are not lawful in the ordinary course of life, nor in any private house; and therefore neither are they so in the worship of God, or in any religious meeting."[1] Basically, Locke would have the State permit any religious practice on the condition that it is a private matter and does not conflict with State's law. In the same work, Locke explains his position in the following way:

> If any people congregated upon account of religion should be desirous to sacrifice a calf, I deny that that ought to be prohibited by a law. Meliboeus, whose calf it is, may lawfully kill his calf at home, and burn any part of it that he thinks fit. For no

---

[1] John Locke, *Letter Concerning Toleration*, 25, https://socialsciences. mcmaster.ca/econ/ugcm/3ll3/locke/toleration.pdf.

injury is thereby done to anyone, no prejudice to
another man's goods. And for the same reason he
may kill his calf also in a religious meeting . . . But
if peradventure such were the state of things that
the interest of the commonwealth required all
slaughter of beasts should be forborne for some
while, in order to the increasing of the stock of
cattle that had been destroyed by some extraordinary murrain, who sees not that the magistrate,
in such a case, may forbid all his subjects to kill
any calves for any use whatsoever? Only it is to
be observed that, in this case, the law is not made
about a religious, but a political matter.[2]

Here, Locke initially declares that his position requires
nothing beyond religious groups obeying the law of the
State. Following this, however, Locke advances an argument
that, having subjugated all religious practice to its law, the
State may prohibit any practice if it be advantageous from
the perspective of secular policy. As the philosopher and
theologian Thomas Storck has pointed out, surely on this
account, for secular reasons, the State may also forbid the
transmission of certain teachings by religious groups.[3] For
if, say, a religious group disseminated moral teachings that
were at odds with those endorsed by the State's schools,
healthcare services, or publicly-funded parades, on Locke's
reasoning there is no obvious reason why the State could
not — or should not — use coercion to prevent such moral
instruction by the religious group in question. (This shift
would be especially likely in States that incorporate into
their law "hate speech legislation," the nature of which is
notably ambiguous.)

That a secular State purports to permit any belief or practice is of little significance if it can legitimately, by its own

[2] Ibid., 25–26.
[3] See Thomas Storck's Introduction to Louis Cardinal Billot, *Liberalism: A Critique of its Basic Principles and Various Forms*, translated
by Msgr George Barry O'Toole and Thomas Storck (Waterloo, ON:
Arouca Press, 2019), xxxi.

lights, quash such belief or practice for secular purposes at any moment. One can easily envisage, on such a model, how religious practices and teachings would increasingly have to conform to the criteria of the State's prevailing ideological commitments. In turn, both from an historical perspective and from that of an abstract analysis, the non-Christian State will always emerge as a counterfeit religious magisterium. The only question is whether, having done so, it will be honest about this.

Given that the highest natural teaching authority, namely the State, when secularised refuses explicitly to recognise the imperatives of religion, its citizenry assume that it is rational for their *appetite for the infinite* — if I may use that phrase — to be transposed onto finite objects. Hence, at best, in such a condition an idolatry of consumerism takes over society, making its members shallow and corroding human culture. At worst, however, the natural religious appetite seeks satiation by a multitude of frustrated and chaotic pseudo-religious causes which erupt into the public arena. Political, ideological, and social differences are then understood not as points for conversation and negotiation, but rather they are viewed through the prism of orthodoxy and heresy. This, in turn, leads to rapid political and social disintegration.

As this disintegration unfolds, in its bid to maintain social stability, the State will naturally attribute to itself final authoritative judgement on religious and moral matters, just as it did in the pre-Christian age. As noted, it will consequently emerge as a post-Christian counterfeit magisterium. Thus, the State will make claims about sex, marriage, family, "selfhood," when innocent people can be killed, and progressively, which opinions it is permissible to hold in one's cloistered conscience. The State will increasingly interfere with every aspect of its citizens' lives, implicitly believing its own bureaucratic system to operate as a quasi-providential hand. The last three centuries of Western history have provided ample examples of the State deifying itself, just as the pagan superpowers did in their most decadent epochs.

Paradoxically, the more avowedly secular, irreligious, or areligious a country claims to be, the more perversely religious it is in fact — just read the following lyrics:

> You pushed away the severe storm.
> You made us believe.
> We cannot live without you.
> Our lands cannot exist without you!
> Our future and hope depend on you.
> Even if the world changes hundreds of times,
> People believe in you.

These are not the lyrics of an evangelical Christian song about Jesus Christ. This is a North Korean anthem about Kim Jong Il. Human beings will always worship, and that impulse to worship will always find expression at the political level. Either, then, the government will endorse and safeguard conceptions of religiosity that are chaotic and idolatrous, and thus corrosive and immoral, or it will endorse a religiosity that results in the genuine moral unity of the State's members.

The only reason why we assume that the political arena *can* be secular or religiously neutral is because in the West we were, until comparatively recently, a Christian people. Christianity had claimed that political leaders could not ordinarily possess competence to interpret its doctrines nor diffuse the means of sanctification, and hence it required apostles and their successors. Ever since we abandoned the Christendom model of religion's connection to politics, we have entered a long epoch of competing ideologies. These ideologies always rest on whatever is deemed to command our deepest and most profound longings. At times, ideologies have rested on vague notions of "progress" and the "universal brotherhood of humanity," while at other times they have been based on more concrete objects, like nationhood or ethnicity. More recently, new ideologies have focused on promises of accumulated commodities and the satisfaction of sexual yearning. Every one of the muddled ideological systems that has informed the structure and direction of the modern State has been nothing more than a counterfeit religion of a people claiming to be emancipated from religion.

No sooner will a government claim to be religiously neutral than it will adopt the most fanatical doctrines and practices — as is widely observable today in the post-Christian victim-worship of Western countries and their adoption of liturgical processions and months of festivity in celebration of mere sexual confusion. Moreover, governments will claim powers of encroachment and intrusion hitherto considered unthinkable, treating as heretics those who do not endorse its new religiosity in public, and now increasingly in private.

Just as Christians were persecuted by religious governments for the private practice of their own religion in the Church's early centuries, so too are Christians beginning to be persecuted by allegedly religiously neutral governments today. In many instances in the West, moral judgements based on theocentric or natural law conceptions of human flourishing have already become criminal offences. The coalescing of persecution advanced by "private" organisations at the behest of the State, with rising identity-based hate crime legislation to rout dissenters from our midst, has fully revealed the fiction of secular or neutral politics.

Granted, there is arguably a moral duty for States to coerce and punish in defence of what they judge to be the overarching truth of human existence and flourishing. My point is that we should at least be honest about this. But the modern State is not honest about this; it claims to be secular when it is in fact intensely religious, and its confused religiosity will only intensify in the coming decades.

Christians have always believed the devil's claim that all the kingdoms of this world belong to him (Matthew 4:9), for which reason Christ called him the "prince of this world" (John 14:30), and St. Paul called him "the god of this world" (2 Corinthians 4:4). Hence, Christians hold that the State will either be discipled and belong to the Kingdom of

Christ — a kingdom which does not have its origin in this world (John 18:36) — or it will exist as a fiefdom of Satan's principality (John 14:30). Either way, it will possess one or the other's species of religiosity. And that is why Christians hold that there is an imperative to make disciples of all nations (Matthew 28:19).

We ought never to ask ourselves the question of whether religion and government should be separate or admixed, since separation is in practice an impossibility. The only question is: what kind of religion do you want your State to endorse, and consequently to impose upon you?

# ❦ 4 ❧
# PATRIOTISM AND
# NATIONAL IDENTITY

ETHNIC IDENTITY AND NATIONAL identity are two principles that have always sat uncomfortably together in my life. I was born and raised in England, and yet my surname has a suspiciously Mediterranean ring to it. If Morello is English, it is English like Rossetti or Disraeli, not like Browning or Thatcher. My great-grandfather, Juan-Battista Morello was a Gibraltarian merchant of Italian, probably Sicilian, ancestry. He came to England at the end of the 19th century and married a woman of Welsh heritage named Mary Davies. Their son, my grandfather, whose name was Carlo Arturo—though he would only be known as Charles Arthur—married a woman the ancestry of whom is unknown, for she refused to speak of her family, childhood, or upbringing.

Their son — my father, Robin — married Yvette Mazierski, the daughter of an English woman and a World War II refugee from Poland. Their son in turn married a Romanian immigrant; I live in Bedfordshire with my wife and half-Romanian children, permanently perplexed for I understand only half of everything said in my home. I love my family, but if we were dogs we couldn't be shown at Crufts. This is my ethnic identity. And yet, were you to ask me of my *national identity*, I would tell you that I am English, and not only English, but intensely English. I love this land, its people, its countryside, its customs and traditions, its pubs with their tepid beer, its ancient institutions and tacitly settled way of life — all that we used to call a *constitution* before the 18th century ruined the word. The personal tension I have felt between national and ethnic identity is, I believe, based on a mistake.

It is undeniable that the political Right has at times exhibited the tendency to root arguments in the principle of ethnicity. This was always deeply flawed and ill-fated. Interestingly, this tendency cannot be found among the early conservatives who so fiercely reacted against the tsunami of revolution in the 18th century. Read Burke, Maistre, Chateaubriand, Bonald, or the later Cortés, and you will find a great deal about nations and constitutions, but little or nothing about race and ethnicity. Indeed, Burke was an Englishman of Irish ethnicity, and Maistre was a French-speaking Savoyard of Italian ethnicity.

I suspect that race-centred themes in right-wing politics arose from a transposition of the Left's obsession with abstract categories — to which the concept of race lends itself — and the conception of nationhood framed as ethnic purity by the so-called "Enlightened Despots." If I am correct about the origins of such currents, then we can be sure that these have no home with or in the political traditionalism which I advocate.

Race-based arguments in defence of national identity have a certain arbitrariness to them. Afterall, why skin-colour and not something else? Furthermore, such arguments do not lead to any conclusive answers about the role of the nation and the duties of its members. There is also a pragmatic point: arguments rooted in racial identity, when posited by conservatives in defence of the nation, simply cut them off from making any contribution to mainstream political discourse, rendering them sterile. Conservative-minded people, over time, have wholly moved away from the topic of ethnicity in seeking to defend such principles as nationhood, civil duties, the integrity of the family, the social role of religion, and so forth. Fascinatingly, with this ideological territory unoccupied, the Left have moved in, increasingly rooting their political, social, and cultural positions in matters of identity, including ethnic and racial history. Plausibly, this development in the Left has only brought forth bad fruit.

The "right-winger" who maintains that race is important to account for his political or social views does so only to possess something symbolic of his feeling. After all, it would be surprising if he who says that Britain is only for "white people," for example, when asked to specify his affection for his country, responded that it really is the pasty complexion of its members that he alone cares about. His fixation on pale skin marks an attempt to maintain something symbolic of what he deems under threat. The question, then, is *what* is it exactly that is symbolised in his mind by pale skin? His divisive opinions on race may be indefensible, but what they represent may be wholly defensible. And perhaps such a defence of the underlying principle is the only way to vanquish its unsavoury expression.

Obsessing about race indicates exactly the kind of materialism of which conservatives historically have been suspicious. For this reason, I consider one of Sir Roger Scruton's achievements to have been the re-rooting of patriotic feeling and national identity in a principled moral disposition. This emerges early in his career. In his 1980 book, *The Meaning of Conservatism*, he wrote the following:

> Every society contains the seeds of a constitution, in the form of custom, tradition, precedent and law. But it may have to fight to preserve these, and from every successful fight a degree of "nationhood" emerges. For most of us the state means, not just government, but also territory, language, administration, established institutions, all growing from the interaction of unconscious custom and reflective choice. The nation state is the state at the extreme of self-consciousness. It has its territory, its people, its language, sometimes even its church.[1]

The nation, then, is not something made by the State, or magicked up by a document or a committee, but a moral

---

[1] Roger Scruton, *The Meaning of Conservatism* (Basingstoke: Palgrave, 2001), 174.

unit that unfolds out of history, of which the State is the eventual political formation. Certain themes come to the foreground in this work, which were developed throughout Scruton's life. For him, patriotism comprises prejudicial feeling and affections. The patriot desires to settle in this territory established and ruled by law, and do so by making a little part of this territory his own, whence comes the importance of property.

What flows from this is the theme of being someone of somewhere, rather than anywhere or nowhere, a theme upon which Scruton bestowed the name of *homecoming*.[2] Furthermore, patriotism is displayed in respect for the longstanding institutions of the nation, including the political process, the courts, the royal family, and so forth. Most importantly, patriotism is seen in the pursuit to understand, and lay claim to, the cultural inheritance of the nation. The true patriot, for Scruton, is someone who has discovered the nation as a treasury from which to make life rich, bequeathed to the living by the dead, one day to be given to those yet to be born.[3]

These themes, however, do little more than specify the phenomena. It is not enough to know what patriotism comprises; we must know what *accounts* for patriotism, its underlying principle. It is in seeking to answer this question that Scruton developed the idea in his 2014 book, *How to be a Conservative*, of the "first-person plural of settlement."[4] This is the "We" of the nation. Patriotic expression is accounted for by the human capacity to lose one's individuality in relation to the nation and its members: to see oneself as part of a "We," a people with whom one belongs, and without whom one is lost.

The first-person plural of nationhood is certainly essential in the Scrutonian schema. But some years ago I attended

---

[2] See Roger Scruton, 'Homecomings' in *The Roger Scruton Reader*, edited by Mark Dooley (London: Continuum, 2011), 185–208.
[3] The so-called "Burkean Contract"; See Burke, *Reflections*, 194–195.
[4] See Roger Scruton, *How to be a Conservative* (London: Bloomsbury, 2014), 31–40.

a colloquium on the thought of Scruton during which the atheistic philosopher and writer Raymond Tallis queried: what is it exactly that distinguishes the conservative's "We" from the revolutionary's "the people"? Tallis noted that persecuted dissenters in the USSR were, when liberated, often overjoyed to discover their respective individuality, no longer to be only politically identified with the "We" of *the people*.

There are of course certain important differences between the "We" of the communist or revolutionary, and the "We" of the conservative. When Scruton speaks of "We," he speaks of one's immersion in the moral unit of the nation, that prepolitical entity identified with civil society, and not directly with the State. The State, from the revolutionary viewpoint, is the author of society, not its mere political expression. The communist sees exactly the same world as the conservative, but he is standing on his head. Nonetheless, Tallis raises a point which requires a deeper response, one we find in a later development of Scruton's thought.

A new theme emerges in the later writings of Scruton, namely the notion of *second-person perspective*. It is embryonically present in *The Uses of Pessimism* (2010), again in *Green Philosophy* (2012), and finally developed extensively throughout *The Soul of the World* (2014). The nation is a moral unit, it is a "We," and yet that "We" is composed of "I"s.

Basically, for there to be a "We," I must see you not as an object but as another subject with whom I am in a certain union — with whom I can share a vision. My fellow countryman must be understood as a subject who is engaged in the same project, who is trying to understand my perspective and trying to have his perspective understood by me. In this way, there is a "We" only because there is a You — that is, another *I* who is to be afforded the respect due to a reasonable person with serious concerns worthy of proper consideration.

Second-person perspective, as the proper disposition of the nation's members in relation to one another, is essential for any kind of democratic participation. I have plenty of reservations concerning democracy as a dominant political form, and indeed I'm sceptical about how well it is currently working in most of the world. Be that as it may, democracy, or something approximating it, is what we have. And as things are, I can only accept the winning of an election by a political party I deem contemptible because I operate on the assumption that those who voted with the majority have the same desire as I do, namely *our* flourishing as a people. For this reason, I more or less accept the outcome of the election, opting to wait it out until the next one rather than riot or begin a civil war as a fitting expression of my discontent. One of the chilling characteristics of the progressive is his inability to see his political and cultural opponent as another subject, another "I," and hence to grow violent when politics appears to be on the "wrong side of history," as his preferred phrase would have it. Rather than another subject, the conservative-minded person is seen by the progressive as a malign object which must be eradicated, not reasoned with.

From the Scrutonian viewpoint, the second-person perspective is the proper disposition of the nation's individual members. What, though, of the relationship between nations? Had Scruton lived longer, I like to think he would have developed the theme of the capacity of persons to possess second-person perspective, and that he would have developed this in such a way as to encompass *corporate persons*. Nations, as corporate persons, are distinct moral agents, and as such may be commended or blamed. They are also capable of maintaining their individuality, their distinct cultural and political character, whilst seeing themselves as part of a fraternal project with other nations. This, I should point out, cannot be achieved merely by the assumption of distinct nations into a super-state arrangement or any other global political union, which in turn would only corrupt the national distinctions presupposed by the union in the first instance.

We can try to understand how the second-person perspective functions among nations by having recourse to the analogue of the family. My family is a moral unit — that is, a corporate person in its own right. The love its members have for the family as a whole does not diminish the affections they have for other families. Our family, as a whole, desires to see the flourishing of other families. Such kinship between my family and other families does not require some contract entitling their members to freely move in and out of our home without any restrictions. Still, we want to be close to other families, we want to collaborate with them, we want to celebrate their special occasions like birthdays and organise fun events together. The suffering of other families is something we wish to prevent, and their flourishing is something we want to secure. It is worth noting that were we (or they) to adopt a child, none of this would be changed, whatever the ethnic background or skin-colour of that child.

If the identity of a nation's members is to be rooted not in the dead-end principle of race, but in the moral disposition comprising affection and gratitude towards a particular territory and its people, then this leads to a rather controversial position regarding the issue of "cultural appropriation."

Cultural appropriation, that great sin of our age, turns out to be the fundamental prerequisite for the cohesion that brings about a sense of national identity. The topic of cultural appropriation was raised by Scruton in 2018 during a conversation with Jordan Peterson at an event hosted by the Cambridge Centre for the Study of Platonism. Scruton observed that his whole life had been based on appropriating the culture of the English aristocracy, into which he had not been born.

The willingness of the immigrant to appropriate the culture of the land to which he has come is precisely the disposition required to prevent him from falling into pariahdom. Recall the words of Ruth the Moabitess to her Israelite mother-in-law: "Where you go I will go, and where you lodge I will lodge; your people shall be my people, and your God my God; where you die I will die, and there will I be buried" (Ruth 1:16). There has never been a more enthusiastic cultural appropriator than Ruth, that holy embodiment of affection and kindness.

The perpetuation of isolation from the wider culture among immigrant communities throughout England, communities which have never shaken off that feeling of being strangers in a foreign land, has had terrible effects, not least of which has been the providing of new recruits to terrorist organisations. Perhaps such undesirable consequences could have been avoided had we treated cultural appropriation as a virtue rather than a vice. It is difficult to imagine a tweed-clad young man, walking a spaniel and whistling the tune of *Lincolnshire Poacher*, arriving home and opening his laptop to enrol in a new caliphate's militia over an ale and ploughman's. Cultural appropriation indicates that gratitude and affection are present in the individual, which is precisely what is necessary for his or her participation in the national life.

So too, we may say that a nation's appropriation of aspects of another nation's culture is an indication of national second-person perspective — i.e., one nation's desire to see things from the viewpoint of another nation, at least in part. (For example, albeit a trivial one: it is simply perverse to perceive something offensive in England claiming curry as its national dish, which it does.)

What emerges out of this picture of national identity and the moral disposition required for its attainment is something entirely consistent with Scruton's definition of "conservatism." I once asked him to summarise conservatism in a single sentence, to which he responded that he could do it with a single word: love. True conservatism always seeks to unify, affirm, treasure, understand, *conserve*. It belongs to the impulses of the revolutionary to divide, tear down, protest, reject, repudiate, destroy.

Scruton recognised that ethnicity-based arguments were — to use a metaphor employed by Lord Tennyson — moulded branches that should be lopped away. Establishing anew the cause of national belonging by situating its defence in the moral life of the nation's members was one of Scruton's achievements. Any conservative movement of the future

would do well to concentrate on this facet of his philosophy.
Part of the first stanza of Tennyson's poem, "Hands All
Round," wonderfully summarises the ideas I have sought
to convey in this chapter:

> First drink a health, this solemn night,
> A health to England, every guest:
> That man's the best cosmopolite
> Who loves his native country best.
>
> May Freedom's oak for ever live
> With stronger life from day to day:
> That man's the best Conservative
> Who lops the moulded branch away.

# 5

# AGAINST A NATIONAL LOYALTY DIVORCED FROM THE SACRED

THE CONSERVATIVE PARTY LOST THE national election in 2024, leading to the Labour government of Sir Kier Starmer, not because of the popularity of the Labour Party but because of the contempt in which the Conservative Party had long been held by its own traditional voters. It will be interesting to see whether the United Kingdom enters an age of more "populist" politics. Many thoughtful small-c conservatives have grown wary of populism: the fleeting success of Boris Johnson marked the Tories' flirtation with the populist paradigm and just look at what the country suffered under that unprincipled oaf. Had a Labour leader botched Brexit like that and then placed the country under house-arrest, he would have been accused of advancing a socialist experiment and hounded into hiding. Johnson—"the people's Prime Minister"—got away with it simply because of the populist mythos that had been created around him. "He must be on our side," so many thought, but of course he never was.

In the UK, the old conservatism is on its way out; populism hasn't yet got a foot in. If it were no more complicated than that, perhaps a simple solution could be found to the crisis of traditionalist politics, at least in these isles. But increasingly, conservatives are questioning what it is they're meant to conserve, when so much seems to have been swept away by relentless social repudiation. Then, of course, there are the subdivisions of "civilisational conservatives," "Christendom conservatives," "Enlightenment values conservatives," and the "individualist, free-marketeer conservatives," all of whom hold irreconcilable conceptions of conservatism. So, what is the future of conservatism?

Among younger conservative-minded people, I've noticed two camps emerging as some workable vision of a future traditional politics is sought. Loosely speaking, there are those who look to *ethnic identity* on which to build the conservative case of the future, and there are those who look to the land itself. The former emphasises ethnic bloodline, homogeneity, and the importance of recognising the dynamics of human tribalism; the latter emphasises the land, shared territory, and the sense of belonging that dwelling together in a single locality brings about. Making such principles into exhaustive foundations for a future small "c" conservatism will, I suspect, lead what is left of such conservatism down a cul-de-sac.

But what the new conservative debate, which is largely a "Gen Z" debate — mostly online — has revealed is that we are expected to side with one or the other of these camps. The former think that the kind of shared territory we have is largely an effect of the ethnic community that has dwelt there for centuries, if not millennia. The latter think that if you dwell in a certain locality for long enough, it will shape you, and certainly it will shape the generations of whom you will be just one ancestor. At bottom, these budding conservative visions attribute to different sources a certain causal power for the establishment of something approximating nationhood.

Those who look to the land think that those who emphasise a shared ethnic identity are going to ruin any future for conservative arguments in the public arena by tarnishing them with what is, in their view, basically racism. And the former equally think that the latter are going to ruin any future conservative case by rooting it in non-scientific, empirically flimsy sentiments that amount to a belief in "magic dirt" — a phrase coined by the so-called "alt-right" pseudonymous writer Vox Day. As the previous chapter suggested, I am concerned that conservatives might go down the path of racism in attempting to root their cause in some foundational principle. I have attempted a personalistic case for national identity, for it has long been my hope that conservatives would help to bring an end to the 20th century's obsessions, not perpetuate them ad infinitum.

It seems to me that both groups are actually appealing to some sort of providentialism. Both think that as a nation comes about, it develops a kind of value — or to use the 18th century term, a *genius* — that is precious and must be protected. This emergence of nationhood should be seen as a gift, and induction into its ways should be viewed as the sort of initiatory passage from which our very sense of selfhood arises. Both groups are anxious about defending something that they deem to have intrinsic value.

I am inclined to sympathise more with those who look to the land. Anyone who has rambled across the English landscape knows that the earth itself possesses a kind of sacrality that radiates forth into the souls of those attuned to its frequency. Unashamedly, I believe in ley lines and other cosmic energies that run through the earth, I believe that certain places have spirits that guard and protect them, and I also think that the saints — whilst beholding the face of God — dwell in the very places that they consecrated with their prayers and sacrifices during their lifetimes.

All that is to say, I believe that the world is a magical realm that theurgically participates in the celestial liturgy of the Godhead, but that this cannot be known by some intellectual ascent out of the world of experience. Rather, it can be known only by encountering reality in its most concrete, gritty actuality. I believe in the enchantment of the skylark's song and the night-time constellations, in the dance of the spheres and the upward hanging fungal fruits that might nourish or kill you. I believe that the interpretation of the earth that belongs to the desert cultures of the Middle East, however noble, is different to that which gave rise to *Piers Ploughman* and the works of Shakespeare. I believe in magic dirt because I believe in both magic and dirt, but I also believe that we are formed by that magic dirt — that it possesses a very potent causal power — and having been so formed we have become something unique and precious.

A French Jesuit named Charles Bourgeois reported a conversation he had witnessed in the 1920s on Poland's eastern border between a Polish nobleman and a Belorussian priest, the former being Roman Catholic and the latter Orthodox.[1] The nobleman opined that in the life of the Christian what mattered was the learning of catechism and the habit of personal prayer; the Orthodox were, in his view, too attached to ritual and liturgy. Fr. Bourgeois recounted the reply of the Orthodox priest:

> Among you it [the liturgy] is indeed only an accessory. Among us Orthodox (and at these words he blessed himself) it is not so. The liturgy is our common prayer, it initiates our faithful into the mystery of Christ better than all your catechism. It passes before our eyes the life of our Christ, the Russian Christ.

I do not introduce this anecdote to suggest that there is some necessary Christian case for any future political traditionalism, even if at bottom I do in fact think precisely that. This chapter, though, is not the place for that argument. The point of this anecdote — for my purposes, anyway — is that for the priest, his source of meaning did not spring from a set of abstractions or concepts, but from the traditions that incarnated his source of meaning in the place in which he lived. The only Christ he knew was the Russian Christ. So too, the only Christ the English should *know* is the English Christ, the Irish Christ among the Irish, the Polish Christ among the Polish, and likewise and so forth for any given people.

And it seems to me that it is the underlying assumption of the Belorussian priest that should be that in which any future political traditionalism ought to be rooted, namely that a nation and its territory are correlative principles that together make up a corporate person — who can truly make the claims of a person. And just as the life of any person is

---

[1] This account is taken from Geoffrey Hull, *The Banished Heart: Origins of Heteropraxis in the Catholic Church* (London: T&T Clark, 2010), 51–52.

sacred, so too the national life of this corporate person is sacred. As with any sacred thing, it can be desecrated.

In the winter of 2023, I flew to the U.S. for a debate with a rising academic on the future of liberalism. During the long flight over the Atlantic, I watched a documentary entitled *Lakota Nation vs. United States.* In many ways, it was a ghastly film, with all sorts of garbage drawn from half-baked critical race theories (the climactic moment of the film was a Lakota Nation march of witness, in which the viewer is shown the ridiculous spectacle of Native Americans in traditional dress waving rainbow and "trans" flags). Nonetheless, the film's merit was in its presentation of the historical struggle for the Black Hills that stretch from western South Dakota into Wyoming, and the intense feeling that this most sacred of mountain ranges for the Lakota Nation had been directly desecrated due to the greedy seizure of it by the U.S. government. Well, equally, I want to suggest that the transformation of England by mass immigration and the colonisation of ancient cities and towns by people who want England's spires to stand in the shadow of minarets should be felt by the English to be a desecration of something both gifted and holy.

This is where, it seems to me, the conversation should be had: given that a nation is a natural good, that emerges providentially down the centuries, and may be considered a "sacrament of nature" (in the idiom of Thomas Aquinas), should it be treated as possessing a kind of sacrality of its own? If so, I submit that all discussion of the good of the nation should be centred on this principle. Such a principle is not eccentric, for even the most reductionist, materialist right-winger raises concerns about unregulated or badly regulated immigration and the rapid transformation of his culture because his nation is at least sacred *to him.* I am suggesting that we treat such a sentiment as reasonable *communally.*

And this, I submit, is the *real* problem with the type of leader we have today. Take a look at Westminster. Listen to what they say. Take time to listen to their speeches and interviews. These people think exclusively in terms of efficiency, outcome, and productivity — if they think of anything besides their own private ambitions. Nothing to them is sacred in itself, and that is why, according to my analysis of where the conversation about the future of nations should rest, generally speaking such people have absolutely no business being political leaders.

Ever since Prime Minister David Cameron launched his "Well-Being Report" in the early 2010s, according to the Report's criteria Northern Ireland has been consistently the happiest place in the UK. Yes, you read that right: the UK's most economically deprived, religiously divided, war-torn region is also the happiest. How can that be? Well, Northern Ireland is a patchwork of extremely tight-knit communities living amid a spectacular landscape, and over 50% of the people attend church every Sunday (compared with 4% in England). Essentially, the Northern Irish are still sufficiently traditional, rooted, and communitarian enough to be happy, and they still renew those attachments in a covenant with God each week. Hence, the UK government's own report on well-being condemns the entire individualist, efficiency-based paradigm of "human flourishing" that our politics perpetuates.

Until the conversation shifts into one that orbits the sacrality of what Roger Scruton simply called "homecoming," we will be stuck where we are, namely with a politics of empty promises about immigration in the face of widespread frustration, on which nothing will be delivered because one eye is kept on GDP. The frustration with which such politics must contend will continue to oscillate between a now dichotomised "blood or soil" narrative, both of which seem a dead-end. Neither GDP, nor ethnicity, nor material conditions should be our *primary* focus, however important they may be as secondary considerations. Rather, the public conversation of the future must centre on the *sacrality* of place and the particular people who dwell there, and in turn the possibility of desecrating that place, against which there is a moral duty to be on our guard. All the politics of the future must become, and necessarily will become, mystical, for the alternative is oblivion.

# 6

# CHRISTIANS SHOULD WELCOME STRICTER BORDER CONTROLS

A FRIEND TELLS ME THAT IT IS ONLY "good intellectual hygiene," as she puts it, to explain from the outset how one is personally implicated on any given topic. In turn, I wish to admit again that to which I have already confessed: that I am almost entirely a product of immigration into England. In my family we have Italian, Spanish, German, Polish, French, Ukrainian, Welsh, Scottish, and Jewish ancestry, and additionally I am married to a Romanian. We even have a good helping of English blood thrown in there for good measure. We are, it is clear, a family of mongrels. Hence, as a political philosopher, as a practising Christian, and as an ethnic Heinz 57, the question of nationhood and national belonging is of pressing concern to me personally.

So, first, what does Christianity have to tell us about nationhood? According to the Bible, salvation came through a chosen nation, the nation of the Israelites. Thus, nationhood plays a central role in the story of salvation from the beginning. The Israelites, we should remember, were in a deeply antagonistic relationship with all surrounding nations. But in Christ's sacrifice on Calvary, God founded a New Covenant, for which He gives what is known as the Great Commission, namely for Christ's new community — the Church — to go forth and make disciples of all the *nations* (Matthew 28:19). Hence, in the New Covenant, God replaces the antagonism of the Old Covenant with a fraternal vision of nations as belonging to a supra-national family, historically called Christendom. Such a fraternal vision, however, does not eliminate the need for national distinctions, but presupposes it.

Nationhood, far from being at odds with Christianity, is at the very heart of its teaching on how Christ's redemptive mission must unfold. In this context, the case for nationhood must not be confused with the ideology of *nationalism*, which denotes the pathology of treating the nation as some kind of idol. And certainly, the Christian teaching on nationhood does not entail a strictly binary conception of nations that would see no possibility for someone of one nation to join another. Indeed, after the ascension of Christ, the head of the Church, Peter the Apostle, emigrated to Rome; Thomas to India; James to Spain; Mary Magdalene to France; and most importantly, Joseph of Arimathea to Somerset.

As mentioned earlier in this volume, even in the Old Testament, we find the figure of Ruth the Moabitess, who having married an Israelite, says to her mother-in-law: "Where you go, I will go . . . your people shall be my people, and your God my God" (Ruth 1:16). Ruth, then, is the cultural appropriator *par excellence*.

Cultural appropriation — widely considered a great sin in our age — is in fact what is required to conserve national identity during times of population movement. The willingness of immigrants to appropriate the culture of the land to which they come is precisely the disposition needed to prevent them from falling into pariahdom and adopting an insulated, ghetto culture. It is to this issue of cultural appropriation that I will return, for, above all, I am convinced that the reason immigration has become a primary political issue in recent years is because the large number of immigrants coming to the UK have generally been very poor cultural appropriators. Hence, at the time of writing, according to a YouGov tracker, 61% of Brits feel that immigration is too high, and one cannot help but wonder how many of the remaining 39% belong to immigrant communities. But more on that in a moment.

But for now, I only want to convince you that Christianity accepts and supports national distinctions. The vision of fraternally related but distinct nations which we call

"Christendom" was the most enduring social order in history. Christendom's ideal of fraternal charity between nations, though often falling short of that ideal, was nonetheless observable in *inter*national collaborative projects such as the creation of hospitals and universities, as well as the offering of refuge to members of neighbouring countries in times of war or persecution, and the ransoming of slaves captured by north African pirates from the 9th–16th centuries. (As it happens, I have often wondered if Morocco should pay reparations to the Cornish . . . but I won't hold my breath for that.)

The standard vision of our civilisation, founded on the high ideal of interpersonal charity — or *agape* — between the corporate *persons* of the nations, was a massive achievement, even if always imperfectly realised.

Christian charity, however, is not the same as sentimentalism or superficial emotion, nor does Christian charity neglect to consider the harmful effects of otherwise good intentions. So, let us consider a few things that are not only *not* required by Christian charity, but may be altogether contrary to such charity.

It is not charitable to incentivise people from other countries to make treacherous journeys in unstable vessels, often having to pay extortionate rates to criminal trafficking rackets. It may be retorted that the number of people approaching our shores in such vessels remains relatively small, but that is to miss why the public conversation about immigration has increasingly focused on such arrivals, namely because the small vessels are now *symbolic* in the British mind of a situation that has spun completely out of control: the regulation of who comes into the country.

It is not charitable to drain struggling or war-torn countries of their younger and often more economically privileged members, who leave at home the underprivileged population who don't have the means to travel or pay traffickers, to then struggle in rebuilding their lands with fewer human resources.

It is not charitable to incentivise young men to make a new life for themselves, leaving behind the women and children in the lands they've fled — for it has not gone unnoticed that (at the time of writing) 90% of those recorded arriving on our shores in small vessels are male, with 75% of them aged 18–39.

It is not charitable to disrupt gravely the lives of settled people, by, for example, placing large numbers of newly arrived young males in economically deprived areas of the UK, where routinely vulnerable British girls of disadvantaged families are preyed upon. (In fact, it is noteworthy that these large contingents of immigrants are never placed in the protected villages of the Cotswolds, for example, where so many of our political class have their second homes.)

It is not charitable to flood British towns and cities with recently arrived populations, throwing into disarray the settled way of life of those communities, many of whose members have been there for centuries. For example, it is *wrong* that the English people of Leicester — who still comprise 35% of that city's population — should watch their city turn into a battleground for hysterical militias of the Hindu and Muslim inhabitants, as happened in very recent history.[1]

It is not charitable to cripple economically the already struggling UK taxpayer in order to direct an eye-watering £1.3 billion per year into housing immigrants in hotels, many of whom have entered the country illegally.[2]

It is not charitable, when facing those with legitimate concerns about our current immigration policies and the lack of consultation of British communities that are being adversely affected, to shout "bigot" and "xenophobe" — phrases that have long been deployed to quash any public conversation about what is going on in our country.

Since 2004, more people have arrived in the UK each

---

[1] In August and September of 2022, the city of Leicester, in England's East Midlands, saw a period of religious and ethnic tension, routinely erupting into ongoing violence, between the city's Hindus and Muslims. The unrest reached international headlines.

[2] See *Cost of housing asylum seekers in hotels*, https://www.migrationwatchuk.org/briefing-paper/509/cost-of-housing-asylum-seekers-in-hotels

year than in the entire period between 1066 and 1950. Brits have concerns that are wholly legitimate regarding this rapid transformation (some would say, destruction) of their indigenous, British culture — concerns that would be roundly deemed entirely reasonable were they expressed by any other people on the planet. Even referring to the English as the indigenous people of England is sufficient to cause many of our powerholders to froth at the mouth. For some reason, which remains obscure to me, one gets the impression that the people of these isles are the only indigenous people without a right to exist.

Do the points that I have raised entail that *all* immigration is problematic *per se*? Well, I hope not, given that such a case's widespread acceptance would likely mean the expatriation of my own wife, which could introduce some tensions into our marriage. In any case, that is not my concern; my concern is rather the more basic and prior question of whether we, as Christians, should welcome *stricter* border controls.

Obviously, there is no hard and fast rule when it comes to this issue — and it's no good trying to appeal to some supposed "innate right" either to conserve one's nation or to join another nation. Rather, one must consider what a concrete settled people are prepared to accept in their shared territory. And *that* is an ongoing conversation. That conversation will largely be determined by the historical epoch, the relations of *that* people with populations of other countries, the type and quantity of immigrants who wish to come and settle, and the unwanted or — conversely — the desirable consequences of such immigration.

But that conversation was for decades shut down by our political and media elite, and now in recent years the frustration has so mounted that people are insisting on having this conversation even if it means exclusion from polite company. Having insisted on this public conversation, people have discovered that, all along, they belonged to a silent — or silenced — majority.

And this brings me back to the matter of cultural appropriation. Speaking very generally, it seems that a key reason
why immigration has become a primary political issue in
recent years is because the large number of immigrants who
have come and continue to come to the UK have proven
themselves to be very bad at cultural appropriation.

My grandfather, Janusz Mazierski, came to England, aged 5,
as a Polish refugee during World War II. He arrived with his
mother Stanislawa, and they were later joined by his father
Roman, after Roman was liberated by the Allies from the
concentration camp where he had hitherto been imprisoned.
By the end of the War, this penniless immigrant family had
put down roots, and they knew they would not be going
back to Poland. England was now their home. Thereafter,
they sought to induct themselves into English society and
appropriate English culture. My grandfather won a scholarship to Dulwich College, later trained as an architectural
engineer, and spent his life designing and building houses
in Kent. In that county, he purchased a farmstead, where
he enjoyed shooting gamebirds and keeping horses. My
grandfather always treasured his Polish pedigree, and yet in
early adulthood he applied for — and was granted — British
citizenship, a status of which he remained immensely proud
for the rest of his life.

That little story presents a very different attitudinal stance
to that of so many immigrants in Britain today. Just visit
Birmingham, Luton, or Bradford. Entire cities no longer
appear British at all. People coming to Britain, not learning the language, not embracing the established culture,
and forming ghetto communities which eventually swell
to encompass whole towns and cities, all betrays an attitude that was utterly objectionable to my Polish grandfather,
who strongly believed that one should only seek to settle in
another land with the kind of gratitude towards it that he
both felt and exercised.

Whilst it is certainly true that many who are concerned
by immigration are worried by the sheer numbers, I think

they are predominantly concerned by the concrete effects: their country no longer feels like their home. Just as the Israelites were promised a land in the Old Testament, so *every* nation has a moral claim to enjoy its land, which, after all, is its only home.

British people — especially the English — increasingly feel that their home has been, and is continuing to be, taken away from them. It behoves Christians, who believe in nations and national territories, to invite a thoughtful and dispassionate conversation about how, practically, we might undo this damage and prevent further damage — and not to accept terms like "bigot" and "xenophobe" to be thrown around in the face of very reasonable concerns.

## PART II
# ENGLAND AND ITS NEIGHBOUR

## 1

# DELAYING THE END OF ENGLAND

## ON ENTERING THE
## LITTLE PLATOONS

I N A PARK IN THE TOWN IN WHOSE outskirts we live, there is a garden. It is a beautiful garden, and it is there for no other purpose than to beautify the rest of the park and the lives of its visitors. The small trees, the plants, and the many flowers change throughout the year, selected to survive the seasons, being continuously tended by a small team of middle-aged ladies and gentlemen. These people are volunteers. They do not live near the garden, and they are unable to enjoy its blossoms apart from during those visits to its beds when they bestow their careful attention.

This group of volunteers, week-in week-out, mind this garden for the benefit of everyone else, and they are rarely — if ever — thanked by their countless beneficiaries. The garden is a true "common good." It is not a "private good," enjoyed only by one or few individuals. It is not a "shared good," that can be divided up among a certain group, vanishing in the process. It is a common good, for the degree to which someone enjoys the garden is not the degree to which others don't enjoy it. And in fact, the more one enjoys it, the more enjoyable it is for everyone else. In this way, the garden is metaphysically superabundant — though I don't think the gardeners would put it quite like that. The garden is also completely pointless. Or rather, it has no point beyond itself. It contains within itself its own purpose. Thus, it is one of the most important things in the town, for whilst most things are *means*, this garden is an *end*.

It is increasingly typical for those who are worried about the future of their societies to talk of a great conspiracy of the "deep state" against the people. Such anxious commentators, however, rarely see that — whether there is a "deep state" conspiracy or not — *they* are more likely the problem behind their society's ills than corrupt pin-striped politicians plotting in secret basements. Society *is* disappearing, and it won't be salvaged by winning arguments in the comments sections of YouTube videos. The only way to save society is to immerse ourselves in it for the good of everyone else. Infinitely more counter-revolutionary than the internet-reactionary complaining about the deep state cabal is the gardener in the park.

Unfortunately, young people do not join clubs and associations anymore. They are content to intensify their solipsism by associating with others only through the portal of their social media accounts. Membership, *true* membership, by which a community's members mingle and become part of each other's lives, is a retreating feature of our existence. The young internet-reactionary is all too inclined to assume that he can transform his society, moving it towards what he thinks would be better, and that he can do this by distancing himself from that society and standing in judgement over it — judgement frequently expressed in cynical and sneering Tweets. This, however, is to take the easy way out.

It is commonly observed by the Right that the leftist's great sin is that of loving humanity. Humanity is easy to love, for it demands only an inner feeling and no more. In truth, one ought to love one's *neighbour*, who is likely almost insufferable. On the other hand, the internet-reactionary's great sin is to bemoan the disappearance of his civilisation whilst making little to no effort to induct himself into what actually remains of it, with a view to revitalising the rest. He doesn't join the local council, or become a member of the local historical society, or the village woodland trust, or a bellringer for the parish, or a whipper-in for the beagles. He thinks the real battles happen online, whilst the *actual* society that he claims to want to save has been abandoned by him.

Last summer, I saw, in the most striking vision, what a vigorous society can bring about. I found myself at a window seat on a flight back to England from Italy. For the few hours this flight lasted, there wasn't a single cloud in the sky. I read nothing, and I didn't sleep a minute. I just watched as the Old Continent passed by beneath. I admired the great lakes of northern Italy, the colossal teeth of the Alps, and the vast landscapes of France. As the aeroplane flew over the north of France, however, I was astonished by the sheer ugliness of the land. All the way to the horizon, as far as the eye could see, was a great beige grid. Rectangular field after rectangular field, comprising one massive Excel spreadsheet of arable industry. If I were asked to visually represent the rationalist, Napoleonic, codified modernity that the French forced in different forms on most of the world, I could find nothing better than the industrialised farmlands of northern France.

Then, France was left behind, and over the Channel we flew. My heart leapt as the white cliffs emerged across the briny. From above, the English countryside was a marvel to behold, especially in comparison to the unbeautiful parcels of agricultural rationalism of moments earlier. I suddenly understood why French novels are urban and English novels are bucolic (apart from those of Dickens, who gives us a solely hellish vision of city life anyway). I gazed in wonder at the swirling fields that followed the contours of the land, the hedgerows, the woodlands, the coverts and copses, the canals, and rivers. The English countryside, far from a grid, was more like a great medieval tapestry, full of colour and surprise. England's rural community, I saw, had evaded rationalism and found sanctuary in spontaneity.

Why was it, I thought, that England's countryside looked this way? It is because — until recently, in any case — we have not treated our landscape as a mere provider of food only, but as the guardian of a way of life. Our coverts and copses are filled with gamebirds that we shoot for sport and gobble at Christmas. Foxes and hares, the traditional quarry of those who hunt with hounds, also need these hideouts to escape the pack and keep the chase sporting. The canals and rivers are lined with fishermen in fair weather, a rare climatic occurrence treated with reverence by the English. The woodlands are full of deer (more prevalent today in Britain than at any time in recorded history), whose venison is treasured throughout the land. Ramblers and hikers have pressed for more footpaths, and the countryside is deemed a good — a *common good* — for all those who like to visit and rediscover that they are not, after all, robots. Farmers are rightly jealous of their lands, and yet they routinely do their part in maintaining the footpaths and bridleways, because they know better than anyone that England's countryside and its inherited culture are indivisible.

In short, rural England looks the way it does due to the English genius for institution-building. Yes, there are the grand institutions like the monarchy, the two houses of parliament, the inns of court, and so forth. But there are also the "little platoons," as the Burkean phrase goes: all those little societies, clubs, trusts, associations, communities, and unions that make up English society. The farms, the hunts, the shoots, the fisheries, the ramblers' associations, the countryside trusts, and all the little bottom-up, organic "platoons" of membership that are so normal to the English have made the landscape the spectacle that it is.

On the Continent, it is common for people to live in apartment blocks at the centres of cities and large towns. Many of these buildings' apartments are almost palatial, and I have enjoyed generous hospitality in many of them during my travels. Continental Europeans do not seem to mind living close to one another, or knowing more than just the names of their neighbours. It is a moral defect of the English that they so keenly guard their privacy. (No doubt this trait comes from our inordinate affection for bourgeois culture, and our egalitarian discomfort with public, aristocratic culture — which is just another way of saying, our *envy*.) Every Englishman wants his own house with its own garden and a fence going all the way round — a cheap substitute for the moat that he'd prefer. Our beautiful countryside is always, therefore, under threat, as the sprawling suburbs of urban centres increasingly grow with each man insisting on keeping his own "castle."

The English have negotiated a way of maintaining the privacy that they hold sacred, and simultaneously preventing the complete atomisation of society: they have emphasised civil association. The English genius for institution-building is what has conserved the English nation, rather than allowing it to become a mere island of detached houses with each household declaring itself a nation in its own right. England has survived by becoming a land of little platoons, of communities of people who bind themselves to one another whilst respecting the privacy that they've come to enjoy. This has been, in some ways, a huge achievement. The outcome, though, entails that if the platoons die out, so does England.

The lack of interest found among the young in joining and perpetuating such "platoons," then, is very worrying. That modern phenomenon, alongside the volume of immigrants coming to England who have little interest in its culture and history, or in adopting the ways of life that have made England what it is, may mean that what is left of real England will soon be snuffed out. If Blighty *can* be salvaged, that will not come about by accruing a certain number of "likes" on social media or squabbling in a YouTube comments box. Those who long to restore our society and lay claim to our cultural inheritance must step into the square and make it their own. There is no other way.

# 2

# COMMON CULTURE
# AND IDENTITY

## ON SURVIVING AS A PEOPLE

I N *NOTES TOWARDS THE DEFINITION OF Culture*, T.S. Eliot argued that all high culture is in fact low culture or folk culture, or in the terminology of Eliot, "common culture," that has been elevated and transformed.[1] Thereby, it has become universal, not by losing its local character but by making its localism universally accessible. As it happens, the more intensely local high culture is, the more universally accessible it is. Consider Shakespeare, whose Englishness is stitched into every word of his marvellous plays and exquisite sonnets, even those whose settings are distant lands or mythical places. It is Shakespeare's utter Englishness that makes his work universally enjoyable. The same goes for all the masters of our high cultural canon, from Dante, who is so perfectly Florentine, to Goethe, the archetypal German polymath.

A decade and half before Eliot developed his argument, Ralph Vaughan Williams made a similar case in his *National Music* lectures, published in 1934, in which he argued that all great music was folk music that had been transfigured and raised up for the international arena.[2] We should take note of the arguments of Eliot and Vaughan Williams, for we have a crisis in high culture precisely because we have a crisis in common culture. High culture has largely ceased to be *cultural* at all, and this has occurred because we have

---

[1] See T.S. Eliot, *Notes Towards a Definition of Culture* (London: Faber and Faber, 1948).
[2] See Ralph Vaughan Williams, *National Music and Other Essays* (Oxford: Oxford University Press, 1987).

substituted our local folk cultures for so-called "pop culture," which is no culture at all. Thus, we have a crisis in high culture because we now have little or nothing to transform.

The high culture that we inherited from those who built the civilisation that we are now dismantling has, in turn, become increasingly instrumentalised for the sake of activism. This trajectory is seen in the way we approach our great high cultural achievements, achievements whose content we do not understand and to which we can no longer contribute. Some years ago, my wife and I went to see Macbeth, performed by the Royal Shakespeare Company. During the play, one of the three witches departed from the script in order to deliver several novel lines comparing Macbeth's increasingly tyrannical leadership to the presidency of Donald Trump, to whom the witch referred by name, to the applause of the largely bourgeois audience. A few years later, we thought we would give the RSC another chance, and went to see their biographical play about Caravaggio entitled *The Seven Acts of Mercy*, which turned out to be an extended work of propaganda, re-educating us on the "systemic injustices of a hierarchical society." I thought we were going to learn about the chaotic life of one of the greatest Renaissance masters, but I was again left disappointed.

Why, I am compelled to ask myself, can we not just enjoy *art*, and relish the brilliance of our high cultural inheritance — which, after all, is our right, since it is *our* inheritance — without being subjected to propaganda and progressivist activism?

The fact is, we do not know how to cope with high culture now, because we were never inducted into culture *per se* through a locally shared common culture. The essence of high culture, which is *meaning*, and which bridges the local and the universal, cannot be grasped because that from which it is a bridge is not understood or even experienced. In turn, high culture has been instrumentalised for progressive ends and has ceased to be high culture at all.

The recovery of common culture, or folk culture, or low culture — whatever you want to call it — is an absolutely paramount imperative. Common culture is the foremost force that can be communally owned, shared, and advanced, that prevents people from being remade as objects of pure use and reduced to mere cogs in the great machine of modernity. If we want to avoid the new global slavery that is so quickly emerging, we must protect that which is ours, that which is not a means to anything but an end — and that is exactly what culture is. Culture is an *end*, being that for the enjoyment of which we labour.[3] Some years ago, I became acutely aware of this fact via a particular sequence of events.

My two older children were in a dance show held on a Saturday afternoon in the auditorium of a local high school. My son, then aged four, was dressed in yellow and black stripes and sprang about on the stage with a group of similarly dressed children to Rimsky-Korsakov's *Flight of the Bumblebee*. My then six-year-old daughter, with her ballet group, performed some dances from the coda of *Swan Lake*. There were sixteen dance performances in total. An enormous amount of effort and work had gone into organising the dances and looking after the attendees, who were treated with homemade cakes and cups of tea by volunteer caterers at the interval. For what end had this taken place? There is no answer to this question, for the entire event was an *end*. It was just for the sake of itself.

Days later, a number of May Day celebrations were taking place nearby. We went along to a local festival. There, Morris dancers performed with their handkerchiefs, sticks, and bells amid a clapping crowd, games and competitions were enjoyed, a great hog roast was served with lashings of apple sauce, young children with ribbons in their hair danced around the Maypole while onlookers knocked back locally-brewed ale, and a local lass was crowned and adorned with flowers as she was proclaimed "Queen of the May" and paraded around on a wicker throne to the cheers of the multitude. Again, why were we all doing this? For the sake of it.

---

[3]  See Josef Pieper, *Leisure the Basis of Culture* (San Francisco: Ignatius Press, 2009), 19–74.

Later in the month of May, we attended a nearby country fair. Youngsters of the Bicester and Whaddon Chase's pony club — tomorrow's fox hunters — demonstrated their equestrian competence in a fenced-off arena, the huntsman exhibited his foxhounds alongside foot masters with their beagle pack, and rare breeds of sheep and cattle were shown to admiring merrymakers. Wandering around the markets at the show, we bought some chips, and I tried the local beer. We also struck up a conversation with a beekeeper who was selling large tubs of honey taken from his hives, and he did very well out of us.

A week later, from shore to shore, the country was covered with Union Jacks as Her Majesty's subjects celebrated her Platinum Jubilee. We drove into town on the Jubilee weekend to witness the jubilations. Army and Navy cadets were firing various kinds of artillery in the main park, and merry-go-rounds and tea-cup rides had been set up on the pedestrianised high street. Near the Market Cross, a singer with a wonderful voice, spectacularly outfitted in a long Union Jack dress, sang old hits — mostly from the 1940s — whilst a local society of swing dancers twirled around the square. The crowds were too much for me, so I snuck off to a pub for a pint of the nearby brewery's excellent oatmeal stout while the wife and children listened to the singer. (I was pleased to escape just as an inebriated lady moved into the middle of the square to cut some shapes that no doubt looked wonderful to her, but to her alone.) I was informed later by my wife that the singer, before concluding her performance, sang the national anthem, at which everyone present stood with hand over heart.

All these events were *ends*. A huge amount of hard work went into them, and a great many volunteers were required for each, and all *for the sake of it*. Events like these teach us that we are not human doings, but human beings, and we only *do* that we may *be*. One of the terrible features of modernity is that we measure everything by the criteria of productivity and consumption. But we were not made to be productive, nor even to be successful, at least not as our world understands such terms. We were made to flourish.

Historians believe that the medieval peasant, for all the difficulties he may have faced, laboured for no more than 150 days per year. So, what on earth was he doing for the other 215 days of the year? He was making a culture. He was participating in religious processions, playing instruments, singing songs, having parties, brewing ale, helping to build the local church, competing in games — in short, he was doing that for which he laboured the other 150 days of the year. In other words, he was living.

Computer games and television shows can never substitute for the genuine and wholesome leisure that we need. We need to be together, in community. Such leisure, real leisure, is always local — that is why it arises symbiotically with common culture. Common culture is always local culture, which is why the "global community" cannot have a common culture, and has required the development of an anti-cultural counterfeit called "pop culture." Since pop culture is for the "global community," it must appeal to that which is most universally accessible, and therefore available to the lowest common denominator. Were pop culture not to do this, it would undermine its own universality by its moderate exclusionism. Pop culture must, to succeed, appeal to that which is lowest. In turn, pop culture appeals to base appetite.

Initially, pop music, for example, was characterised by the simple three-minute song about fairly innocent feelings of affection for a member of the other sex. These songs were always problematic, as they were short (to cater for short attention spans), they simplified the complex impulses of the heart, they veiled certain moral dangers, they reframed self-realisation in terms of appetitive pursuits (albeit innocently portrayed, at first), and the music itself increasingly privileged rhythm over harmony and melody, thereby prioritising that dimension of music that speaks most to the passions. Now, half a century or so down the road, the vast majority of pop songs are explicitly pornographic in content and their accompanying videos — with all the bottom-shaking and sticking out of tongues — well correspond to the songs' contents.

It is important to understand this trajectory, because the global monoculture of *pop* has been promoted for a new global community by the *globalists* — all for a reason. Those who want you to be a slave will enslave you first by way of your appetites. It is very difficult to control a man who already governs himself. It is very easy to control a man who is a slave to his own appetites, for he has already fettered himself. Joseph de Maistre well explained this in *Du Pape*, arguing that societal slavery follows interior slavery.[4] Maistre claimed that slavery always existed because it is *natural*, and the only way to get rid of slavery is to make it *unnecessary* by the accomplishment of personal self-government among the citizenry. The choice is before us. Pop culture is appetitive and will facilitate universal enslavement; common culture is wholesome and will foster local liberties.

It has been widely noted by conservative commentators that we are rapidly moving into a meaning-based political and cultural discourse. Everything from the success of Brexit to the rise of "woke" indicates that the discourse of the coming epoch will centre less on the economy, or property rights, or any other talking point of the 1980s and '90s, but on *meaning* and *identity*. Essentially, the emerging discourse will be shaped by what John Vervaeke, Professor of cognitive science at the University of Toronto and now also a successful YouTuber, calls the "meaning crisis." At bottom, this means that the emerging discourse will focus on *ends*.

What do we want from our shared civic life together? What is our culture? What is our identity? Who are we? What do *we* believe? These are the questions now tormenting the West, and they are not going to go away. Whether we are enslaved or emancipated depends on what answers we give to these questions, and what practical measures follow

---

[4] See Maistre, *The Pope*, 238–245.

from such answers. This is why the local events which I described above are of such importance. They may sound quaint and twee to the modern reader, but they are exactly the things that teach us who we are as a people. It is out of such communal activity, enjoyed as an end and not for the sake of anything else, that what Roger Scruton called "the first-person plural" of a people emerges.[5]

Let's take stock for a moment.

Much suggests that the dollar will crash in the coming decade. Our food industry is probably on the brink of collapse. We are currently witnessing the fall of the American empire, which probably has less than half a century left. Other economies, partly due to the astoundingly imprudent response to COVID, are set never to recover. We are watching the emergence of new imperial and colonising powers, none of which appear to have civilising motives. The future may belong to China, but not for long given that they — like most of Asia, Europe, and the Anglosphere — are heading into a demographic catastrophe that is now inescapable.

Our governments have no coherent vision and remain utterly unequipped to offer a moral and practical vision for their nations. The same governments are ramping up the control of their citizens and are using highly technologized — and in many cases unlawful — means for greater control. We only have a shadow of a society, given that marriage and the family have been almost completely corrupted. In recent times, children and young adults have been queuing up to have their genitalia mutilated, and their guardians are not only not protecting them but encouraging them. The leading cause of death in the West among teenagers and adults up to their mid-thirties is suicide. There has never been such distrust between the sexes. Due to the aforementioned demographic decline, Europe's settled peoples will soon hardly exist. Great Britain is successfully keeping its numbers up by having almost no effective immigration policy, allowing

---

[5] See Scruton, *How to be a Conservative*, 31–40.

an intake of around 100,000 immigrants per year of people who largely do not understand the ancient constitution and culture of this little island, nor want to.

Our ecclesiastical institutions, which should be the first to successfully engage in the emerging meaning-based discourse, are cesspits of moral and financial corruption, filled with faithless and self-serving clerics who are falling over each other to appease the world and its prince. Our leaders are ceasing to lead. Our universities are ceasing to teach. Our courts are ceasing to apply the law. Our Churches are ceasing to sanctify.

In short, we are completely unready for what is coming. And the oft-suggested conservative solution of forming "parallel communities" is not much of a solution at all. It is into your society that you were born; it is to that society that you have obligations; it is that society that must be redeemed; it is to that society that you have a mission. Of course, it isn't clear how we will weather the coming storm, but it *is* clear that we'll have to weather it *together*. No society, no survival.

So, how do we survive as a society? Well, for now, gathering as local communities for the sake of wholesome festivities isn't a bad place to start. It may seem like a small thing, but without such small things you cannot even know who you are. And the question of *who we are* is fast becoming the chief question.

## ⚛ 3 ⚛

# ENGLAND'S CONSERVATISM
# AND THE GLOBAL REVOLUTION

I T IS DIFFICULT FOR ONE WHO DOES NOT live in England to fully appreciate how deeply conservative are the instincts of the English. Indeed, one of their national peculiarities is that they are perhaps the most proficient exporters of revolutionary mayhem—and always have been—and yet such noxious ideas and their effects rarely, if ever, gain a foothold in England in the way they do abroad.

It is possible that these English characteristics of instinctive conservatism and tacit revolutionary enthusiasm can be traced all the way back to the medieval period. At the height of the High Middle Ages, John Wycliffe launched in England his proto-Reformation, the Lollard movement. The divisions and dissentions entailed by his ideas, however, were felt on the Continent as they laid the blueprint for the Hussites, who in turn broke up the unity of religion throughout Bohemia. In England, however, Lollardy was quickly suppressed, with the coronation oath of the monarch thenceforth incorporating a promise to protect the kingdom's religion from such heresies in the future. Such an upheaval could not be stomached; that was simply not how the English did revolutions.

William of Ockham, with his nominalism, anti-papalism, and prideful voluntarism, made few ripples here. Abroad, however, his views made a pope rage, delighted an emperor, and seeped into the German academy. Eventually, his thought became entangled with other currents which were popular at the famous University of Erfurt. There, such ideas made the already cantankerous friar and professor of theology, Fr. Martin Luther, increasingly disturbed, until he not so much discovered a solution as *willed* one into existence. As the pandemonium escalated, the English across the Channel continued their merry lives unalarmed.

The instinctive conservatism of the English, which dictates that even revolutionaries must look like conservatives, has always been chief among their traits. In the 16th century, the English were unable to accept Protestantism — or rather, have it forced upon them, if William Cobbett is to be believed — unless it was packaged as the same sort of thing as Catholicism.[1] The English were happy to accept Luther's doctrine, whose content they did not know, as long as they still had their bishops, priests, high liturgy, sacraments, choral tradition, and all sorts of ecclesiological "branch theories," so that they could pretend that nothing of substance had happened to their Church. In short, England accepted the Protestant revolution on the condition that it was neither very Protestant nor very revolutionary.

There were of course those who wanted a *real* religious revolution: the Puritans, eventually led by Oliver Cromwell. They wanted no bishops, no priesthood, no sacraments, and no sacral monarchy — and they won the war with which they cursed their country in pursuit of destroying such things. And yet (because it is England we are talking about), within a generation the established Church enjoyed remarkable stability, and the son of that holy king whose head they'd lately chopped off, was sitting on the throne.

Of course, despite having got their throne back, the Stuarts did not last long. England soon had its political revolution in 1688. And yet, Edmund Burke opened his famous work, the *Reflections*, by making the argument that the so-called "Glorious Revolution" was really an unremarkable continuation.[2] Given that Mary — daughter of the Stuart king, James II — took her father's throne with William of

---

[1] See William Cobbett, *A History of the Protestant Reformation in England and Ireland* (Charlotte, North Carolina: TAN Books, 1988; first published in instalments from 1824 to 1826).

[2] See Burke, *Reflections*, 85–122.

Orange, Burke suggested that the hereditary principle had been *upheld*. Only in England would it be necessary, when toppling a royal dynasty in an act of revolution, to also argue that the hereditary principle had been championed and the royal line conserved.

We English brought forth the Baconian mechanistic worldview, perfected by Newton's universe, and yet the transposition of such instrumentalism, rationalism, and materialism into a political movement was left to the revolutionaries of France, whilst political organicism was largely maintained in these Isles. With John Locke, we issued the ideals of a religiously neutral polity and the notion of a new national contract based on "self-evident" moral truths, but it was left to the American colonists to realise such a vision in their revolution.

Bentham and Mill swept the rug out from under the feet of received moral norms, concocting a radical liberalism, but these ideas took off elsewhere — the staunchly religious "conservative" liberalism of Gladstone alone was accepted within the Establishment here. Progressivist ideas were all the craze among Victorian romantic darlings, and yet leading such enthusiasts as William Morris and members of the Pre-Raphaelite Brotherhood simultaneously affirmed the moral framework and aesthetics of a vanishing Christendom.

In England, Marx and Engels developed their materialist dialectic, writing tracts that announced imminent liberation for the oppressed proletariat, before they filled their crystal saucers with vintage Moët and rode out to foxhounds. Their ideas went abroad, inspiring revolutions galore and, eventually, the mass murder of the proletariat themselves — but never behind our white cliffs. No, here the labourite and the socialist were different creatures altogether, and each time their leaders became too radical for comfort, they were swiftly institutionalised with a knighthood or even a seat in the House of Lords. A common trait among our socialists, in fact, was a growing suspicion of communists, whom they saw as corruptors of their cause. Often deeply concerned with local loyalties, cultural heritage, and always intensely patriotic: whether George Orwell or the 1st Marquess of Ripon, here in England one could be both a socialist and more or less respectable.

England eventually underwent the democratisation of its political settlement, adopting the egalitarian delusion and embracing universal suffrage, but it did so without guillotines. England, practically speaking, experienced the same political and social modernisation as every other ancient nation. It did so, however, not with revolts, riots, uprisings, and bloodshed, but over afternoon tea when nobody was looking.

The paradox of the English is that, at bottom, we are instinctively conservative and tacitly revolutionary, and this spirit runs all the way through England. Other countries are pleased to erect guillotines and set up gulags, but we English advance our revolutions with a little more decorum. Hence, we are content to have Lords Spirituals in government, an established Church, and a cross rather than a tricolor on our flag, as long as we can treat our national Church as a joke and fully expect its clergy to do the same. We are happy to have royals if they reign but do not rule; we will have aristocrats as long as they cannot pass on their titles, a parliament as long as it functions as a mischievous oligarchy. We wear tweed jackets and brogued Oxfords while we pave over our countryside and reduce the rural workforce to a single percent of the population. We boast of our Anglo-Saxon liberties whilst living under the world's most extensive surveillance network outside China.

This instinctive conservatism of the English is very dangerous, for by it we believe ourselves to possess a tradition which, like a Georgian terrace, turns out to be all façade. We think we enjoy an organic constitution that in fact has long existed largely as a phantom. We never destroyed our monarchy, beheaded our landed nobility, discarded our representative parliamentarianism, repudiated our religious establishment, or replaced our legal tradition with a *civil code*—but what we did was perhaps more pernicious. Slowly, over the centuries, we took that great civilisational treasury, our common English inheritance, and we reduced it to mere *form* whose content is now much the same garbage as is found everywhere else.

Only the people of this Sceptred Isle would need a "Conservative" government to redefine marriage, extending the marital state to homosexuals and thereby breaking its essential link with reproduction and the nation's future. Among the English, such a radically revolutionary act could only be accepted if it were simultaneously packaged as conservative. As Prime Minister David Cameron put it prior to bringing in the legislation, "I don't support gay marriage in spite of being a Conservative; I support gay marriage *because* I'm a Conservative." Only in England could such a remark make any sense.

We English adopt everything that is procured by revolutions, but we do so without the revolutions. We have thrust ourselves into the nihilistic materialism of modernity and placed ourselves under the same autocratic political management preferred by liberal busybodies as is found throughout the Continent, but we did all this whilst sleeping rather than awake like everyone else.

It did not surprise me that during the COVID hysteria, jabs, masks, ongoing lockdowns, boosters, proof-of-vaccine passes, prohibitions on seeing family and friends, and so forth were all mandated on the Continent. Modern Europe is a monster created by the French Revolution, fostered by Napoléon, and mutilated again and again by that Revolution's demonic spawn, liberalism, fascism, and communism. The EU testifies to its fidelity to this hellish legacy by its refusal to recognise Christianity as the unifying principle of Europe. The people of the Continent are well-used to the choking of society by a State gone awry. Now, when the State says *jump*, the people just ask *how high?*

For this pathetic attitude I do not look down on our Continental friends, for what we English do is much worse. In England, during COVID, we mandated all the same things, but we did so — in the words of the then governing Prime

Minister Boris Johnson — to "protect our freedoms." This is how we do revolutions here. On the Continent, as you chain someone, you at least afford him the respect of telling him that he is now a serf. When you chain an Englishman, you must tell him that the chains are there to make him free.

Many have commented to me that nowhere in the world can you find such liberty as in England. Certainly, "freedom" is now a purely ironic word in much of Europe. Again, during COVID, in Italy for example, one had to be "fully vaccinated" to be permitted to work *from home*. Beyond Europe things were no better. Australia established mass detention camps for the *unclean*, and the freedom-loving U.S.A. became largely a sanitary dictatorship.

The World Economic Forum (WEF) has told us that the world is undergoing a "global revolution," in which the whole of humanity will shift into a new kind of digital universal society, with a digital economy, catering for digital personalities. The virus was seen by the vampires of the WEF as just the thing for accelerating this revolution. As WEF Chairman Klaus Schwab put it, "The pandemic represents a rare but narrow window of opportunity to reflect, reimagine, and reset our world."

I do not like revolutions in any case, but I especially dislike the proposals of the Davos Jacobins. There is, in essence, a moral war taking place between those who see the true realisation of the human being to be that of the actuation of personhood, and those who see it to be that of reduction to a number. It is clear that, in England, we are undergoing this same revolution as everyone else, but we're doing it more slowly and more quietly — as is our custom. You cannot throw an Englishman into a cage; rather, you must have him sleepwalk into it. The English, if they want to avoid the crippling situations in which other nations have already found themselves, and the dystopia that otherwise awaits us all, need to wake up now.

# 4

# THE TRAGEDY OF THE SARUM RITE

A CHARACTERISTIC OF THE MODERN Catholic Church is its liturgical uniformity. Centuries ago, if you were travelling through Christendom, you would have experienced an array of liturgical rites and "uses," all of which would nonetheless have seemed to belong to the same religion. Presently, in the strange ecclesiastical institution that was allegedly born of a "New Pentecost" in the mid-20th century, only one liturgical order is deemed acceptable, the *Novus Ordo* of the Roman Rite—a ritual concocted by Archbishop Bugnini, a shady character with curious Masonic connections.

There's an obvious rigidity among the Church's hierarchs—those senior clergy who routinely conflate uniformity with unity—with regard to what liturgy may be celebrated. And yet going from one church to another often requires a wholesale change of one's religion. This is the case because the *Novus Ordo* allows for such an injection of the priest's personality into the liturgy, that the liturgy itself is frequently a mere platform by which the priest can celebrate his parochial celebrity and his personal opinions on the religion he claims to profess.

For this reason, among others, a growing number of the faithful have sought out the ancient ritual forms of the Church—still offered by certain clergy as part of a sort of underground network—to enjoy liturgy that is actually expressive of their religion, and to escape the self-referential theatrics of the local parish priest. As ever more laity, especially young people, discovered the ancient liturgy of the Church, the Eye of Sauron in Rome turned towards these congregations—and for some time has constructed various means to eliminate them.

Unfortunately, such "traditionalist Catholics"—people previously just called "Catholics"—may suppose that the ancient form of the Roman Rite is the only Latin Rite liturgy that ever existed before the 1960s' "New Pentecost," which successfully emptied the pews in the greatest single apostasy the Church has ever seen. In reality, as I noted above, in old Christendom there were local rites and "uses" everywhere. In fact, liturgical diversity rather tipped over into liturgical chaos, and in the 16th century, Pope Pius V declared that any rite that couldn't be proven to have at least a 200-year pedigree must be abrogated. This requirement was extremely conservative, however, and thus widespread liturgical diversity continued.

In Britain alone, we had the rites of York, Hereford, Bangor, Aberdeen, and Sarum, the last of which was by far the most widespread in these isles. There were also the rites of the religious orders, like those of the Carmelites, Dominicans, Cistercians, and others. Then there were many types of chant, and different styles of vestment, and that's all before we come to low cultural, popular devotional diversity, as almost every village had its own rituals and patron saints. The liturgical life of Britain in particular and Christendom in general was like a great medieval tapestry, full of variety and colour, though forming a single picture of beauty and grace.

Under the lunacy of King Henry VIII, all the rites of these isles were suppressed except the Sarum Rite, which was translated and modified into the glorious but heretical prose of Archbishop Cranmer for use by the king's new church. Later, during Queen Mary I's attempt to restore England to the old faith, the Sarum Rite was re-instituted as the principal liturgy of this land, and indeed she married Philip of Spain in this rite's nuptial Mass at Winchester Cathedral. So, the Rite of Sarum became something of a symbol in the English mind of the old faith's triumph over Henry's invented religion, which he had inflicted upon his subjects with astonishing violence alongside voracious land-grabbing.

It wasn't to last, though. Soon, after Queen Mary's death, this country was forced back into its religious experiments, and the Sarum Rite vanished from the world. Unusually, the liturgical books of the Sarum Rite were preserved, as were books of commentary for the rite. And I'm informed by a respected liturgical scholar in Rome that these books, as well as many copies of them, still exist. Hence, the Sarum Rite in its entirety waits on unvisited shelves to glorify the Living God once more.

There was a reasonable expectation during the rise of Victorian medievalism that the Sarum Rite would be restored to England, and Augustus Pugin — the Catholic convert and architect who was largely the genius behind the rebuilding of the Palace of Westminster — designed all the sanctuaries of his churches to accommodate Masses in the Sarum Rite rather than the Roman Rite. The High Anglicans of the Oxford Movement were especially interested in the Rite of Sarum and sought to bring the use of Cranmer's Prayer Book much closer to this rite.

Evidently, when the English Catholic hierarchy was restored in 1850, there was considerable appetite among both Roman Catholics and "Anglo-Catholic" Anglicans — with many of the latter flirting with converting to Catholicism — for a re-institution of the Sarum Rite throughout England. Pope Pius IX, aware of such appetite, openly gave the newly established English bishops the option of restoring the Sarum Rite, and he pressed the Archbishop of Westminster to adopt it as the rite of his cathedral, which was and is the Catholic mother church in England and Wales. Never, though, underestimate the Catholic hierarchy's aptitude for shooting itself in the foot. In what was a significant own-goal, the bishops rejected Pius's offer. There seem to have been a number of reasons for the bishops' rejection of the pope's proposal.

First, during the times of constant persecution from the 1560s to Catholic Emancipation in the 1820s, the Holy Mass had been provided by a secret network mostly comprising Jesuits and secular clergy trained in France and the Papal

States. Certainly, there was considerable scholarly interest in the Sarum Rite at the English seminary in Douai, France. There, over the Channel, away from the persecution, the Sarum Rite could be more easily offered, which really only comes into its own with deacon, subdeacons, and a host of acolytes all with different functions. But on arrival in Britain there was no possibility for priests to conduct elaborate liturgies; the imperative was to get the Eucharist to the faithful in the simplest way possible. Consequently, the Roman Rite Low Mass — with no music and an absolute minimum of ceremony, requiring only a priest and a single server — was, for numerous English Catholics (especially the old recusant nobility), the liturgy that had seen them through times of oppression and suffering. Thus, perhaps understandably, they were attached to it and didn't want anything else.

Second, among Victorian Catholics there was a culture of passionate ultramontanism, and for many Catholics the faith's distinguishing feature was little more than an intense piety towards the pope. John Henry Newman was an exception in this regard (as in so much else), exercising scepticism towards such borderline papolatry. But even Newman's great mind was insufficient to extinguish the prevailing inordinate obsession with Rome and its bishop. Opting for the pope's rite was seemingly an opportunity for English Catholic bishops to demonstrate their unswerving loyalty to the pontiff, even to the point of discarding their own liturgical inheritance (and that of their flock).

Third, there was a significant desire among the Catholic bishops at the time to look as un-Anglican as possible. For this reason, when the decision was made to build Westminster Cathedral, the hierarchy opted for a Byzantine design over the gothic designs that are associated with Western Christianity, so that no one would mistake it for an Anglican cathedral. Given that the Sarum Rite seemed too much like the rite of "little England," and insufficiently like a rite of the Church Universal, it was apparently held that it was preferable to reject it. After all, it was felt, "little Englander" mentality had been rather too wrapped up with the origins of the English Reformation. Moreover, as so much of the interest in the Sarum Rite was generated through Tractarian scholarship, many Catholic clergy felt that it had already been tainted with the whiff of Anglicanism.

The decision to reject the Sarum Rite was, however, profoundly short-sighted. In Victorian England, there was a widely believed bit of Protestant propaganda that Catholicism was essentially a foreign religion of Irish and Italian peasants. The true English religion was that of the Church of England, people said, the religion protected by the constitution since that gin-bestowing 1688 revolution kicked out the tyrannical, Romanising Stuarts. Anyone with even a superficial knowledge of British history knows how false this narrative really is (notwithstanding that it's still commonly believed due to the historical illiteracy of modern people). Re-instituting the Rite of Sarum would have sent out a message: Catholic Christianity is the English religion, evinced by the fact that Catholics worship according to the liturgy that these isles offered to God for at least five centuries until a strange aberration occurred under the rage of — as Edmund Burke put it — "that tyrant, Harry the Eighth."[1]

Given that there was such interest in the Sarum Rite among the Oxford Movement Tractarians — who by then formed the Church of England's intellectual elite — the Catholic bishops' re-institution of the Rite would have made "crossing the Tiber" for this movement's leaders and their followers very attractive indeed. In short, the rejection of Pope Pius IX's offer marked a terrible missed opportunity for the return of England to her ancient faith.

The good news is, as I noted above, the Sarum Rite and ample commentaries on how to offer it remain in existence. It's all there, waiting to be brought back to the Sceptred Isle once more. And whilst there appears to be almost no cultural interest in this rite among the English today — that

---

[1]  Burke, *Reflections*, 217.

proselytising opportunity really was well and truly missed — it remains part of the religious inheritance of English Catholics and the English nation as a whole. Therefore, there is a moral imperative to restore it. As it happens, permission was granted by Rome at various times — certainly in 1985, 1996, and 2000 — to offer the Sarum Rite for one-off special occasions in England and Scotland. It's been done, and it could be done again.

I would like to suggest some practical steps. First, as the Sarum Rite was of considerable interest to the Oxford Movement, whose heirs are very much the Anglican Ordinariates established by Pope Benedict XVI, the three Ordinariate branches could reasonably claim that the Rite of Sarum belongs to their patrimony and petition to offer it to congregations where there's an expressed desire for it. And second, a priestly society could be established for the Sarum Rite's preservation, perhaps called the "Priestly Fraternity of St. Joseph of Arimathea," named in honour of our Lord's great-uncle and the proto-apostle to Britain. Obviously, under the ecclesiastical regimes to which we've grown accustomed, there is little hope of such initiatives being received with any enthusiasm among the bishops or in Rome, but perhaps when the tide changes a little, such steps may be taken.

# 5

# SACRÉ-CŒUR BASILICA

## COUNTER-REVOLUTION
## INCARNATE

A S MY FRIEND AND I ASCENDED THE steps, the neo-Romano-Byzantine domes of the basilica appeared over the trees ahead, followed by the emergence of the great statue of Jesus Christ pointing to his heart with one hand and with the other blessing the city of Paris. And then, two figures of holiness and chivalric courage appeared, King St. Louis IX and St. Joan of Arc. We had reached the church that I had wanted to visit for over a decade, the Basilica of the Sacred Heart of Paris.

I knelt to pray my rosary before the Blessed Sacrament, and, looking around me, I was struck by the sheer confidence required to build such a place. France, the Church's eldest daughter, in 1789 declared herself no longer a disciple of Jesus Christ but an apostate. She banished the clergy from her lands, slaughtered the consecrated religious, confiscated church buildings and scribbled vacuous revolutionary slogans on their walls, and she announced that Jesus Christ had no rights in the temporal arena. In mockery of the Holy Virgin, a prostitute was placed on a throne and carried through the streets to be installed at the centre of Notre Dame Cathedral and venerated as the "goddess of Reason."

The aristocracy and parish priests, those two courageous defenders of the Church, drawn from the lay and clerical orders respectively, were repeatedly crushed under foot by the new revolutionary State. Soon, this State emerged as the new god of the revolutionary era, which was to satisfy every man's deepest longings as it authored a new civil society in its own image. It was not long before this Leviathan demanded an immense blood sacrifice to confirm its deity. Again and again, the scaffolds were erected, heads rolled, and blood flowed. The Terror replaced the unbloody sacrifice of the Christian liturgy with the new human sacrifices offered to a State that had declared itself the true providential lord of all history, a history that it asserted had come to a close with the birth of the revolutionary epoch.

There were those who opposed the tide of revolution. The people of the Vendée, and the *Chouannerie* of Brittany and Maine, consecrated themselves to the Sacred Heart and marched under its banner, also wearing an image of the Sacred Heart upon their chests. From then on, the Sacred Heart became the recurring symbol of all counter-revolution. Later, the counter-revolutionary Sanfedismo movement of southern Italy was consecrated to the Sacred Heart, as was the Tyrolean Uprising in central Europe against Napoléon. The Carlist movement of Spain, which long sought to defend the rights of the Church in the political arena, always used the Sacred Heart as the image of its cause. In the 19th century, Gabriel García Moreno, founder of Ecuador's Conservative Party, consecrated that country to the Sacred Heart before he was hacked apart by the machetes of Ecuador's liberalist oligarchy.

In fact, the symbol of the Sacred Heart had emerged as a sign of counter-revolution even before the chaos in France. It may be argued that the first great revolt of the temporal power against the spiritual power in the Church was advanced by King Henry VIII of England. This met with a response in the Pilgrimage of Grace, a counter-revolution of nobles, burghers, peasants, priests, monks, and friars, who occupied whole English cities in the North and Midlands in an attempt to re-establish the proper order of the Church polity. The Pilgrims of Grace placed at the centre of their banner an image of the pierced heart of Jesus Christ. The revolutionary character of the King's actions later caused Edmund Burke, in his *Reflections on the Revolution in France*, to compare "Harry the Eighth," whom he calls a "tyrant," to the Jacobins of his own age.

Napoléon, remembering the militias of the Vendée, remarked that, had they marched on to Paris, they could have easily undone the entire Revolution. The problem was that the Vendeans did not want power and prestige, but simply to be left alone to farm their lands and work out their own salvation in the bosom of their parishes. After each victory, rather than marching on, the Vendeans turned back, returning to their families. Therein is a key feature of the traditional-minded man: he is not interested in the political struggle as an end in itself but sees the political struggle as a mere means — and not an enjoyable means — to achieving what he deems really important, namely the humble project of making a home in this fallen world, sanctifying a small part of it that it may be pleasing to his Maker. For the revolutionary, however, life *is* the political struggle, an effort that can be abandoned only at the final eschatological triumph of the Machine of Modernity. And because the men of the Vendée did not dismantle that Machine, it returned to grind them up. A genocide ensued, as Vendeans were tied together and drowned in what the revolutionaries tellingly called "Republican marriages."

The devotion to the Sacred Heart, Jesus Christ had told St. Margaret Mary Alacoque in one of her mystical visions a century before the outbreak of revolution, had been "reserved for the coming age of coldness." As the rationalistic, Cartesian, geometric conception of reality was slowly transposed from the "new science" into competing conceptions of political theory, appetite grew for written constitutions and a top-down, centralised, hyper-statist settlement. Anyone found standing in the way of the great Machine would be offered to it in sacrifice.

It is hard for me to imagine the kind of confidence that would drive French Catholics, after such a diabolical rupture in their once glorious — albeit imperfect — civilisation, to build something like the Sacré-Cœur Basilica. It is as if those still loyal to the old religion one day turned to face their country and exclaimed: *You banished our priests, massacred the brides of Christ, broke up our families, drowned our fellow faithful, confiscated our churches, crushed our liberties, denied the rights of our Saviour and yours, and when we showed you the image of divine love you responded with fire; now, we will ascend Paris's highest hill and there build a great church and consecrate it to that Sacred Heart at which you gnashed your teeth, and the whole city will have to look upon it and weep with shame.*

There, in that amazing church, I prayed for a renewal of counter-revolutionary confidence in the Church Universal. Such confidence ought not to be confused with triumphalism. The French who built Sacré-Cœur Basilica did not do so in a spirit of triumphalism, but of penance. We have little of which to boast. The Catholic Church, insofar as it can be viewed from its institutional, human aspect, is largely a festering mess of doctrinal dissent, moral and financial corruption, scandals of the most heinous and deplorable kind, and one riddled with petty clericalism and careerism. But as St. Paul puts it, "If I must boast, I will boast of the things that show my weakness" (2 Corinthians 11:30). Only in acknowledging our weakness can the healing work of Jesus Christ begin to work wonders, a work of grace from which the only *true* confidence can arise. As the great Machine of Modernity grinds to a halt, as it necessarily will, and probably sooner than we think, we must have the confidence to forsake all counterfeit saviours and rebuild on the only source of true strength: the Heart of the Incarnate Word.

# 6

# ABORTION AS A FRENCH CONSTITUTIONAL RIGHT

I N MARCH OF 2024, FRANCE ENSHRINED abortion as a constitutional right. The scenes from Paris that week were remarkable. In the parliament at Versailles, the new constitutional amendment enshrining adults' licence to kill human babies, either by the use of toxins or by dismembering them and crushing their skulls, was greeted with a standing ovation by politicians. Cheers, laughter, and music were heard throughout Paris as people celebrated this new constitutional "right," which hitherto had been in law since 1975, but was not something that had defined on paper the French State as such.

It is very important for Christians to understand what the political arena is, and why the things we see happening in our age are happening at all. According to the Christian religion, the world belongs to the devil as his principality (John 14:30), all the powers and kingdoms of the world belong to him (Matthew 4:8-9), and as the "god" of this world, as St. Paul calls him (2 Corinthians 4:4), he demands worship and sacrifice. To me, the cheers, the partying, the lit-up buildings throughout the French capital and no doubt elsewhere in the country looked, in essence, a lot like a liturgical offering. The devil is scandalised by the union of spirit and flesh in human nature, he hates the Incarnation by which God divinised human nature—soul *and* body—and thus he seeks to alienate us from our own bodies and warp human nature which has become an icon of God Himself. The devil rejoices in the tearing of human flesh. And just as he did when he was known as Baal, so today he seeks the violent death of babies by those entrusted with their protection, to be a sacrificial offering to him and a recognition of his supremacy in the world.

The Christian response to this evil is not to reject the world and run to the hills, but to capture the world from Satan and offer it to God. For this reason, the Christian apostolate entails the discipleship of nations (Matthew 28:19). The Christian religion and the mission to establish Christendom are, then, inseparable. A great risk comes with the discipling of a nation, however, for if a people later retreat from Christendom and place themselves back under the devil as his subjects, they will become something entirely different to what they were before their evangelisation. Prior to its discipleship, a nation possesses prevenient graces in anticipation of the Gospel. Once a nation becomes an apostate — as France did amid its revolutionary rebirth, as Joseph de Maistre observed with acute perspicuity — by so doing it imitates the devil, rejecting the life of grace, and falling not from light into the shadows, but into utter pitch darkness. This, C.S. Lewis noted in a 1953 letter to his friend Don Giovanni Calabria:

> They neglect not only the law of Christ but even the Law of Nature as known by the Pagans. For now they do not blush at adultery, treachery, perjury, theft and other crimes which I will not say Christian Doctors, but the Pagans and the Barbarians have themselves denounced. They err who say "the world is turning pagan again." Would that it were! The truth is that we are falling into a much worse state. "Post-Christian man" is not the same as "pre-Christian man." He is as far removed as virgin is from widow: there is nothing in common except want of a spouse: but there is a great difference between a spouse-to-come and a spouse lost.[1]

And, if a nation were to lose not only grace but any grasp of the natural order of things, what would it look like? If

---

[1] C.S. Lewis and Don Giovanni Calabria, *The Latin Letters of C.S. Lewis* (South Bend, Indiana: St. Augustine's Press, 1998), 85.

a nation lost not only its sense of obligations towards a revealed Creator but even towards mere natural justice, what would we see? In short, if a nation did not simply become pagan, but overtly satanical, what signs would we behold?

Post-Christian man is not the same as pre-Christian man. Pre-Christian man inordinately favoured the flesh and its impulses, whereas post-Christian man sees the body as a problem to be corrected by technology. We want to "support" women, but we're always coming up against the irritating fact that they have female bodies, so we "support" them by sterilising them and then telling them that mothers are weak and strong women kill their offspring so that they can be useful to wealthy men. The modern age may value "freedom" above anything else, but in many ways, it sees the chief means to achieve freedom to be the tearing of human flesh. Perhaps, then, it is time to abandon our embarrassment about giving this epoch its proper name: the final reign of Satan.

Interestingly, when the constitutional amendment was proclaimed in the parliament at Versailles, and France's politicians leapt to their feet to applaud it, it was announced that this amendment was for the purpose of sending out a "universal message" to "the women of the world" that France would "always move forward by their side." But the rise of abortion politics in the modern world precisely reveals that this world cannot tolerate women *as women*. The modern world, which conflates "progress" and "production" as somehow synonyms, herds women into the competitive workforce, thereby re-forming them as interchangeable units of utility identical to their male counterparts. They must consume toxins to make sure their reproductive systems malfunction so that there is a lower risk of pregnancy (the occurrence of which would certainly identify them as different to men). If a woman *does* become pregnant, she must be able to kill the baby within her. Thus, the entire paradigm eliminates our capacity to treasure women *as women*.

Particularly striking, on that day in March of 2024, was seeing the Eiffel Tower lit-up with the following words: "My body, my choice." These words, like the word "abortion" itself, are clever in their deceptiveness. It is a slogan that can be shouted and seemingly smacks of *progress*. How could anyone possibly argue with it? After all, it's *her* body, and she needs to decide what to do with it. But of course, a body is not a possession. Throw all your possessions into a fire, and if you include your body among them, you will find there's no longer a *you* at all. By our bodies we exist and through our bodies we are related to the world and the people in it, with all the obligations that this entails. The most intimate of such relations is undoubtedly that of the emergence of another embodied person within one's body. And *that* perhaps is why the slogan "my body, my choice" is so deceptive, because the body with which abortion law is concerned, and whose violent destruction it routinely permits, is not the body of the person doing to the choosing at all. Were it *her* body, *she* would be the one being dismembered and having her skull clamped and crushed.

Like so much in the modern world, whether it be "love is love," or "trans people just want to exist," or "my body, my choice," what we have here is something that can be chanted and yelled to avoid articulating the *reality* of what is being referred to. Such deception must be deployed if "progress" is to continue, for the realities that these slogans orbit are so wretched and repulsive that they amount to the stuff of Dr. Mengele's dreams.

Three miles away from the half-burned Cathedral of Notre Dame, a closed off blackened remnant of a dead civilisation, consecrated to a woman who fled to Egypt to protect her baby, the killing of babies was celebrated into the night at the Eiffel Tower. Jubilations erupted around that great metal spike built "in gratitude," as Eiffel himself put it, to the French Revolution and the modern age it inaugurated. Here, at this shrine to "progress," people hugged each other and partied to honour their country for being partly defined by its commitment to the violent murder of human babies.

I do not expect to persuade any pro-abortion reader to rethink his or her position. Even those "on the fence" are not my main concern here. Those who think abortion is a "complex issue" have completely failed to understand the political debate surrounding abortion. The parliament at Versailles did not think it was a "complex issue," nor did the people partying in the streets on the parliament's announcement. Abortion politics is about "progress," and in the modern epoch, the more disembodied we are, the more atomised and alienated we are, the more interchangeable and utilisable we are, the more depersonalised and objectified we are, so too the more we are, as the progressive's cherished saying goes, "on the right side of history." And for this reason, real marriage and the natural family will always undermine modernity, and hence cannot be tolerated, let alone treasured. Modernity must emancipate us from, as Simone de Beauvoir pithily put it, "menstrual slavery."

For those who call themselves "conservatives," however, it is probably time to rethink what we mean by the current "emerging conservative alliances." Open your eyes: in France, the so-called "far-right" parties all supported the constitutional enshrinement of abortion. If you are a Christian, then those parties are your enemies and should be condemned by you as such. Those who traditionally called themselves "conservatives" are being made hypocrites by so-called "conservative parties." A radical response is required, something quite different to that to which we've grown accustomed.

Conservative or "right-wing" politics cannot treat issues like abortion as "areas of reasonable disagreement." If it is now somehow "conservative" to exercise indifference towards the killing of babies, or indeed to outright support such murder of the innocent, then to hell with conservatism — literally. Let me be clear: I would rather progressives increase their global usurpation until we are all living under a single tyranny of interminable "progress" than watch Christians support and advance the false witness of a pro-abortion political "conservatism."

It grieves me to say it, for I was formed in the crucible of Burke, Maistre, Bonald, Donoso Cortés, Le Play, and other such critics of modernity who really believed that political successes were possible in the modern age. Indeed, I have always believed in throwing oneself into the political struggle, and that in the end conservatives may win out as modernity eats itself. But we must see now that the political changes we witness are mere intimations of a much deeper battle over the territory of the human heart, a conflict which rages on between the Principality of Satan and the Kingdom of Christ.

The conservative-liberal, Right-Left divide means almost nothing now. There are those in the Principality of Satan and those in the Kingdom of Christ, and *that* is really the only division that has satisfactory explanatory power. Of course, there are those who have yet to pick a side, but no one can remain neutral for long in such a conflict. As we come to realise that politics is no longer about the good of the polity, but is the mere expression of a battle between the children of Satan, who wage war on human nature, and those of the God who so loved human nature that he assumed it into his divine personhood, we will have to adopt a completely different approach to our engagement with the "political struggle." It will likely mean not so much being campaigners and activists, but crusaders and martyrs.

# PART III
# TRADITION
# AND
# REVOLUTION

## ⚜ I ⚜

# TEN TRADITIONALIST PRINCIPLES
# FOR THE POLITICAL STRUGGLE

CONSERVATIVE-MINDED PEOPLE ARE lousy when it comes to the political struggle. We don't see ourselves as activists, and we're not very good at adopting such an approach, even as all that is most dear to us is swept away by ideological mischief-makers who know little more than the thrill of repudiating what they don't understand. The reason, of course, that conservatives are poor activists is to be found in the fact that the "political struggle" is not of great interest to conservatives. This is an observation that was well captured in the Viscount Hailsham's *The Conservative Case*:

> Conservatives do not believe that political struggle is the most important thing in life. In this they differ from Communists, Socialists, Nazis, Fascists, Social Creditors, and most members of the British Labour Party. The simplest among them prefer fox-hunting — the wisest [among them], religion. To the greatest majority of Conservatives, religion, art, study, family, country, friends, music, fun, duty, all the joy and riches of existence of which the poor no less than the rich are the indefeasible freeholders, all these are higher in the scale than their handmaiden, the political struggle.[1]

Conservatives want to carve out a small part of this *valley of tears*, turn it into a home, and enjoy their lives in a world that so often thwarts such humble aspirations. For the conservative, the way to do this, as Roger Scruton used

---

[1] Viscount Hailsham, *The Conservative Case* (London: Penguin Books, 1959), 12–13.

often to say, is to cultivate a love for all that is loveable, and forgiveness towards all that is not.

Whilst these observations about conservatives and their attitude towards the political struggle are no doubt true, one cannot raise them to justify complacency in the face of civilizational collapse. We may not be naturally good at the political struggle, but that only means that we must cultivate by art what more degenerate people possess by nature. Basically, we need to learn, and we need to learn quickly.

I hear self-identifying conservatives moan endlessly about the "woke" crowd, when they ought to be sitting attentively at their feet. Woke has re-centred the political and cultural discourse on moral issues, and away from the pragmatism of the 1980s and '90s. Woke has successfully shifted the public debate away from merely economic issues and questions of individualism, and towards what are popularly called "values." Woke has not only re-framed the debate so as to privilege moral principles, but has demonstrated that it is prepared to be socially disruptive and simultaneously colonise long-standing institutions of state and civil society in order to advance its cause. In short, the "woke" crowd have done exactly what conservatives should have been doing over the past decades when they were too busy apologising and conceding evermore ideological territory to their enemies.

Frankly, I'm deeply grateful to the woke movement for re-centring our political and social discourse on moral questions, which is where it ought always to have been. We can lament the gains of woke ideological activists all we like, but they have outwitted us and beaten us at every step. It would have been so easy for it to have been otherwise, given that most people are in fact broadly conservative by nature, but in the face of the woke onslaught we did nothing except cower.

The success of the woke movement is that it has offered a moral and, in fact, spiritual vision of the human drama, and has offered solutions to the unpleasant picture that it has painted of historical oppression and ongoing "systemic injustices," by which it has convinced a vast number of society's members that they are imprisoned and in need of saving. This moral and spiritual vision of the human drama may be all wrong, and deeply noxious to boot, but at least they *have* a vision. It's time for conservatives to wake up. It's time for them to show that they too have a vision — a different, far more fulfilling, and most importantly, *truer* vision. It's time to be socially disruptive, and to retrieve the enduring institutions whilst founding new ones.

Conservative-minded people have to realise that if they want to enjoy the "all the joys and riches of existence" to which Hailsham refers, then they need to be proactive about protecting such wholesome aspects of a life worthy of their love. This means, I'm sorry to say, courting the "handmaiden" of such things, namely the *political struggle*.

I like to live as a hobbit. The things that really matter to me are family, friends, beautiful buildings and rolling hills, poetry, music, good books, good wine, good beer, and good food. Nonetheless, for the hobbits, such simple homemaking was only possible because the Rangers of the North, the Dúnedain, decade after decade protected the Shire from all the orcs and goblins that would have captured it, wrecked it, and enslaved its inhabitants. If conservatives want the joys of Hobbiton, they must engage in the struggle of the Dúnedain.

Below, I offer ten traditionalist principles for the political struggle. This list is not meant to be exhaustive, but it offers a concise overview of commitments that any conservative-minded person ought to keep before his mind's eye as he battles the orcs that torment him:

1) **Do not conflate *ends* and *means*, or you will fail.** There is a terrible tendency among conservatives to treat liberty as an *end*, rather than a *means*. If there is any immediate take-home lesson not only from the rise of woke but from the COVID experience, it is that the vast majority of people will readily sacrifice many freedoms and liberties for some *good* that they judge to be an *end*, and thus superior to their

freedom. If all you can offer people are means, with no vision for what life ought to look like when such means are used, then you deserve to lose. Conservatives need to advance a coherent moral and spiritual vision for the human person if they are going to engage in the emerging "meaning-based" public discourse. You must argue for an *end*, namely human flourishing in the existent and organic communities by which we have been formed, and to which we owe so much.

2) **Redeem the old institutions and found new ones.** Conservatives should approach the old institutions, especially legal bodies and universities, as the Gramscian activists have done over the past decades. You should infiltrate them, play the game carefully, consciously knowing that you are being subversive towards their prevailing revolutionary cultures. Also, found new institutions. You need a pincer-strategy if you're going to advance your cause, and therefore both approaches are paramount. What you must not do is that which is on the lips of far too many conservatives, namely only establish "parallel communities" where you can supposedly take refuge from the wicked trajectory of the modern world. Remember, fleeing to the hills is what a conquered people do.

3) **Work with all people of good will.** Many people are sympathetic to the conservative cause without necessarily knowing why, or without sharing all the presuppositions or conclusions of more thoughtful conservatives. Do not purposely narrow the number of people who might be your "allies." Those who want to fight against the mob that seeks to destroy our civilisation will rarely agree with you on everything, and there may be some things on which you cannot work together. So be it. The unholy alliance between different schools of revolutionaries is what has made the destruction of our civilisation so easy. Conservatives of different kinds and approaches must work together in a spirit of tolerance. This, in fact, is a part of not conflating *ends* and *means*. As long as you agree on certain ends, you can allow for a plurality of means among you.

4) **Stop trying to look "reasonable" or "nice" to progressives.** They will never like you or tolerate you. The woke, progressivist, revolutionary Left hate you and wish that you did not exist. They deem you an oppressive, colonising, elitist, vile creature because you love God, love your nation, and think children should be protected from relentless sexualisation and ideological manipulation. They think that your interest in history, attachment to your people, and proclivity for respecting what you've received from your ancestors — rather than denouncing and destroying it — is indicative of a bad spirit. They will never respect you. Remember, you are not trying to establish an environment of tolerance and mutual-understanding. They will never allow for such a situation in any case. Like Isabella and Ferdinand, you are trying to recover the territory. Treat the new Left like people who hate you, because they do.

5) **Utterly condemn, in no uncertain terms, the entire LGBTQ+ movement.** If conservatism cannot defend social institutions as basic as marriage and family, then to hell with conservatism. The LGBTQ+ movement comprises the sacred priesthood of the woke religion. From them, the woke crowd receive their doctrine, organise their sacred processions through the cities, adorn themselves with pseudo-sacramentals, and are led in the great offensive of moral revolution. The LGBTQ+ movement is not what it purports to be, namely a movement about emancipation from oppression. Once you have a movement that is extremely powerful, internationally celebrated, has months of public celebration dedicated to it, flies its flag on every important building, can shape ancient institutions as it wishes, controls the education system, and yet still uses the language of victimhood to express itself, you should know that you're dealing with perhaps the most perniciously manipulative revolutionary movement in all history. Forget not: it isn't enough that this movement has corrupted society at its foundations — that is, at the very level of human nature itself — it now seeks to chemically castrate and directly mutilate children. You

must concede absolutely no ideological or moral territory to this movement, and you must work to rebuild what it has already been permitted to dismantle.

**6) Point out that your opponents are both ridiculous and disgusting.** Appearances are more, well, *apparent*, than ideas. Do not think it below you to point out not only what the Left thinks, but what its vanguard looks like. The screaming, swearing, contorted, tattooed, blue-haired, non-binary gorgons that comprise the hardcore adherents of the same ideology to which nearly all our civil servants, charity directors, university academics, and politicians subscribe, indicate how ridiculous and disgusting is the progressive ideology under which we all toil. Never tire of pointing this out.

**7) Treat common culture as an inheritance just as important as high culture, and strive to conserve both.** The technocratic system into which we are rapidly moving seeks to isolate us and turn us all into sexless, soy-eating, grey suited, nationless, middle-class functionaries that can serve any purpose which the regime finds suitable for its purposes. You need to encourage local membership. Join local historical societies, take up hobbies, drink in pubs, attend country shows and fairs, and encourage others to do these things as well. Few want the world that our overlords want to impose on us, but we have all been duped into thinking that it's inevitable. It is not. We can choose what sort of a people we want to be. Doing normal, wholesome activities with friends is a key part of defeating our emerging overlords. For this reason, you must *root* yourself. In turn, alongside this immersion in common culture, read great books, especially the works of our civilisational founding: Holy Writ, Homer, and Virgil. And don't be a snob: remember that common culture and high culture emerge symbiotically. The defence of culture must be at the heart of all conservative activism, and this entails a healthy hatred — which you should never stop expressing — of pop culture.

**8) Defend the family.** For the vast majority of people, there is nothing more important than their spouses and their children. If you defend the family, coherently and clearly, people will join you. One of the first moves of the 18th century French revolutionaries was that of explicitly denying the long-standing rights of parents over their children and declaring divorce legal. The attack on the family has been going on for centuries, and the results have been disastrous, which are now on full display throughout the West and beyond. Progressives have cleverly framed their deconstruction of marriage and family as a mere evolution of an institution that is meant to make it "more inclusive." You must directly criticise this. Parents can now abandon their children with few consequences, homosexuals can rent wombs and buy babies from economically struggling women, online grooming networks can talk children and vulnerable adults into having their genitals mutilated with the protection of the state. What we are witnessing is heart-breaking, and it all begins with the undermining and then the ideological colonisation of the family. Any sound conservative activism must challenge this trajectory, and seek to reverse the corruption of the family, whose destruction is the most sacred cause of progressives.

9) **Explicitly promote a coherent spiritual and moral vision of the human person.** People are crying out for such a vision at the moment. This is the Achilles' heel of progressivism. The entire progressivist movement relies on conservatives advancing no inspiring vision of the human person, and certainly not one that can compete with their vision of the ongoing realisation of Humanity, that intangible spectre that is purportedly being emancipated from its incarnate history and will finally manifest the abstraction worshipped in the minds of revolutionaries. Conservatives used to have an inspiring vision, based on a fallen human nature undergoing transformation via the acquisition of virtues, the development of education, and the formation of culture. Jordan Peterson, for all his unfortunate classical liberal tendencies, has demonstrated that talk of virtue, self-sacrifice, education, and culture really can be inspiring — as

well as get you an enormous following. You should draw some confidence from this.

10) **Do not be embarrassed about making religious claims.** The whole of Western civilisation is downstream from the Christian deposit. In turn, you should be keen to make Christian claims a staple part of your repertoire. We have Greek philosophy, drama, history, and poetry, because these were patronised by the Church when they were repeatedly under threat. We have a sophisticated legal system that takes justice seriously, and naturally resists corruption (but, oh how they've tried), because of the Church's patronage of Roman and Common Law (before these were tampered with by the terrible civil codes of Leviathan). We have rich European folk cultures because these were patronised by the Church, not seen as threatening paganism but as wholesome local attachments that ought to be treasured. The religious illiteracy of the average modern Westerner is very embarrassing. Do not shy away from speaking of the fallenness of mankind and its need for redemption in the discipling of nations. "Whosoever shall be ashamed of me and of my words, of him shall the Son of man be ashamed, when he shall come in his own glory, and in his Father's, and of the holy angels," says the Lord (Luke 9:26–27). Not all conservatives are religious, but all good religious people are conservative-minded, or otherwise they are betrayers who subordinate their religion to ideology. You must be, in the final analysis, in the business of redeeming your civilisation, and hence you should never shy from proclaiming the Redeemer when called upon to do so.

The above are ten *principles*, not rules. That means that they give *form* to one's engagement with the political struggle; they are not a list of imperatives, all of which must be fulfilled. Some of these principles may seem in tension with others. It is difficult to see, for example, how one can explicitly criticise the LGBTQ+ movement (principle 5) whilst infiltrating and retrieving long-standing institutions (principle 2) that have been taken over by progressives. For this reason, I offer an eleventh principle to which all other principles must be subordinated: **exercise prudence.** Realising principle 5, in your own circumstances, may be as simple as not putting a "Pride Rainbow" in your email signature at work, and for others it might mean something more overt. So too, principle 4 (not trying too puppyishly to seem "nice" or "reasonable" to progressives) need not entail being belligerent with all people who have liberal leanings. In your own life, it may simply mean being unafraid to lose friends when you unapologetically voice your own opinions. In everything, prudence — that is the key. With that, I leave you with the words of Gandalf the wizard: "All we have to decide is what to do with the time that is given us." Go forth into the political struggle.

## ⚹ 2 ⚹

# LIBERTARIAN "CONSERVATISM"

### A TROJAN HORSE

THE ONLINE WORLD OF YOUTUBE AND Instagram is filled with short videos of people talking into their phones to deliver a lesson about life to the millions of consumers out there, the worldviews of whom are largely moulded by such half-baked preaching. The worst are the progressives, who usually take a topic associated with gender, sexual liberation, or equality, and begin their videos with some variant of, "I'm just going to, like, explain something to you, okay, for everyone who, like, just can't seem to, like, get this…" Then the person, the sound of whose voice is like a sophisticated Asiatic torture, proceeds to explain to the world her—for it is almost always either a woman or a man with a severe testosterone deficit—moral superiority.

Perhaps the ghastliest facet of such videos is that the airhead talking into her phone finishes each proposition with an upward inflection, as if it were a question. This habit adds insult to injury, as it gives the impression that the self-appointed teacher's ideas are so complex that they must be explained to the viewer as if the latter were a three-year old.

Almost as insufferable as those videos are the ones authored largely in response to them, by right-wing YouTubers and Instagramers. These short videos follow the same format, namely someone talking into his phone to deliver some lesson on what's wrong with wokeness. Some time ago, a friend sent me one such video. Therein, a man is strutting about in a gym, talking into his phone, saying, "If you think you are gender non-binary or whatever, if you want to chop your d*ck off, if you want to go around in a dress and put lipstick on, I don't care; I only care when you start telling my children that they should go do these things…"

This is what stands for "conservatism" in the shallow world of online video conflicts. A woke person comes along and argues for "progress," and a "conservative" then comes along and argues for individualism. And if the debate is going to be framed like that, then I am decidedly on the side of the woke lot. Not, of course, because I believe in "progress," which is an obvious fiction, but because I do not believe in the private individual, which I deem an even more obvious fiction.

Frequently, Jordan Peterson has insisted that the fundamental dichotomy with which the West contends is that of individualism vs. collectivism. According to Peterson, Western civilisation was never built on the maxims of the "Left" or the "Right," both of which he sees as comprising collectivist ideologies. He says that if you're a collectivist, you will eventually end up a socialist, a communist, or a fascist, all of which privilege the community over the individual. One of the central reasons why Peterson criticises whom he terms the "radical Left" is because he thinks these activists are trying to reduce people to mere members of a group in the paradigm of "identity politics," rather than prioritising the irreplaceable individual. For him, then, what is unique about the West is its absolute commitment to the individual.

Peterson is wrong to accept the collectivist-individualist dichotomy. The collectivist-individualist dichotomy is a clear example of the modern mind opposing ideas that are only in opposition once abstracted from reality. What is this collectivism? What is this individualism? I have never encountered a society that was not composed of individuals, and I have never met an individual who did not belong to a society.

Take anyone you know, and try to imagine the pre-societal self that exists there free from all the social influences that have made him. If I try to imagine myself independently of where I was born, the family that brought me forth, the schools I attended, the language in which I think and speak, the books I've read, the friends I've made, I simply cannot do it, and if I were to achieve some imagining of such a pre-social self, it wouldn't be me in any case.

So, what ought the conservative response to be in the face of people living in a way they find reprehensible, if it is not that of doubling-down on individualism? The traditional response — and therefore the response of the traditionalist — would be something like the following:

> We live in a society, and there are some things we will accept and some things we will not, and where the line lies is worked out circumstantially by prudential deliberation and negotiation. We will tolerate certain behaviours which we dislike and be intolerant of others. But if you want to mutilate yourself, we will aim to prevent you from doing so, for we have to live in a community with you, and we think that such behaviour is impermissible in our community. We are not isolated individuals, or even atomised families; we are a society, or at least we must strive to be. We live on streets together, and when you run out of sugar, you should knock on your neighbour's door, and when he runs out, he should knock on yours. We reside together because that's how we flourish. When any one of us lives badly, we *all* suffer. If we each operate as insulated, atomic individuals, with our own private concepts of human flourishing, then the great work of civilisation-building is impossible, precisely because civilisation-building is a shared and common project, of which everyone is a beneficiary.

For the reasons entailed by the above response, conservative-minded people have always valued the city as much as the countryside beyond its walls. Civilisation finds its apex in the polis. (That's why God creates us in a garden that grows up from below, but He glorifies us in a city which descends from above [Apocalypse 21:2–4].) Roger Scruton, in his *Conversations* conducted with the Irish philosopher Mark Dooley, remarked that the city is "the greatest human enterprise after farming — the second step that we took from the world of the hunter-gatherer, and which we took in trepidation and relying always on the help of our gods."[1] It is in the city that we commune in order to build a culture, and we do this partly by maintaining the bond between the urban townscape and the rural landscape.

The city is where people dwell for the purpose of civilisation-building, and that's why the city has always been built around the temple. Numa Denis Fustel de Coulanges, in his magisterial work *The Ancient City*, first published in 1864, writes:

> The city was the collective group of those who had the same protecting deities, and who performed the religious ceremony at the same altar. This city altar was enclosed within a building which the Greeks called pryraneum, and which the Romans called the temple of Vesta. There was nothing more sacred within the city than this altar, on which the sacred fire was always maintained.[2]

The city, then, right from its beginning, was the place of dwelling for those who shared a common conception of who they were, what their purpose was, and how they were to flourish together. They gave the same reasons for their existence, and worked for a common purpose, and did so to please the gods.

As the pre-Christian chaotic expressions of religious craving were superseded by the order and beauty of true religion, we continued to build the city around the temple — that is, around the cathedral and the high altar. But in time the cathedrals were abandoned and the altars neglected, and

---

[1] Roger Scruton and Mark Dooley, *Conversations with Roger Scruton* (London: Bloomsbury, 2016), 89.
[2] See Fustel de Coulanges, *The Ancient City: A Study of the Religion, Laws, and Institutions of Greece and Rome*, translated by Willard Small ([n.p.] Pantianos Classics, 2019), 103.

under the various ideologies that orbited the fictions of individualism and self-authorship, the city became a mere conglomerate of atomic egos in a wallowing condition of alienation, the frustration and malaise of whom are on full display in any modern city.

It is to those very ideologies of individualism and self-authorship that so-called "conservatives" flee in unthinking attempts to slow down the evermore aggressive colonisation of every aspect of life by the forces of Progress. But it is precisely the individualism and atomisation of modern life that has liquefied those sources of meaning that conservatives hold dear. And it is those sources of meaning that liberals think are such a threat to the so-called sovereign individual.

Those sources of meaning — like the family, the village, the nation, the church — are a threat not only because they may be seen as having some authority over the otherwise utterly emancipated individual, but they might also undermine the state's claim to be the *sole* authority over the individual. That's why any unifying sense of meaning is *de facto* unacceptable to the liberal state, which will therefore always privilege the abnormal, the minority, and the alien, and treat with contempt the traditional, the settled, and the indigenous. Hence, liberalism seeks to unify for the sake of progress, and does this by a process of disunification and atomisation. Liberalism is thus a paradigm of political and social schizophrenia, and its adherents display all its internal disorder.

For conservative-minded people, then, to take refuge in the very paradigm which has successfully eroded all that they love and treasure is, from both conceptual and practical perspectives, deeply foolish. Traditionally, conservatism was neither individualist nor collectivist, but intensely communitarian. What conservatives ought to be arguing for is the dignity and irreplaceability of the individual as someone who unfolds out of a community, to which he owes everything. Indeed, the dignity and irreplaceability of the individual could not be known independently of the common good by which he has achieved his relative flourishing.

When a blue-haired, stretched-eared, neck-tattooed progressive insists on subordinating the education system to his own ideological aspirations, the conservative response should not be "Can't you do you, and me do me?" Rather, conservatives ought to accept that they are faced with two opposing conceptions of what a society and what human flourishing look like, and then they should enter into conflict with every hope of winning.

## 3

# CONSERVATISM'S GENERATIONAL DIVIDE

OVER THE YEARS, ATTENDING CON-servative conferences and events both in the UK and abroad, I have detected a divide between conservatism's boomers (those born sometime between 1946 and '64) and its younger people, especially those from the millennial generation (1981–96) onwards. This divide is almost never addressed publicly, but both groups are generally aware of it. They routinely look suspiciously at each other, whilst claiming to be on the same side of political debates and culture wars. Of course, it's true that they share many sympathies in these polemics. Nonetheless, the divide is there, and as time rolls on it is becoming ever more evident.

I owe the conservatives of the latter half of the 20th century a debt of gratitude, for so many of them have formed my own convictions, but I have come to realise that I stand firmly in the camp of the young conservatives, as my age would suggest (I'm a late '80s child). This divide was made clear to me some years ago during a conference on conservatism's future which was held in Brussels, to which I was invited as a speaker. A journalist of the boomer generation was on a panel, and amid the discussion he repeatedly criticised "woke" culture, the trans-movement, and the rise of censorship. Another speaker on the panel, a millennial, challenged the first speaker with suggestions that perhaps we need to think *less* about freedom of speech — and certainly privilege "the good" over freedom of speech — and take more seriously the *underlying* reasons for the civilisational collapse that we're all worried about.

The boomer conservative journalist eventually said that, as he saw things, the imperative was that of restoring the tradition of Western civilisation initiated with the free and open thinking exemplified by Spinoza. Later in the day, when I was invited to speak, I argued that it was precisely with people like Spinoza that we began to see the explicit signs of rot that eventually became the comprehensive decline of our civilisation. "The process of modernity is coming to an end," I claimed, "and it has all been a deeply unhappy story. We cannot refute late modernity whilst defending its origins; it's high time for a full refutation of the entire modern project."

With comments like mine, others inevitably respond, "Oh, so you want to throw away modern medical science, or even your smart phone?" And herein lies the problem. We have deeply imbibed the lie that technological innovation is a correlated principle with moral progress. We think that because we have iPhones, we must be morally superior to our forebears. Thus, we believe we must accept the moral dogmas of modernity, or it might seem like ingratitude for modern medicine and telephones. In fact, it is precisely because modernity's moral dogmas have been enforced alongside technological innovation that the latter has been such a colossal danger to us all. One only needs to question with some seriousness the thought that technology has brought about moral betterment to be disabused of such an error.

This, it seems to me, is what accounts for the fundamental divide that exists between typical boomer conservatives and typical young conservatives: the former believe that there is at root nothing fundamentally wrong with the modern project, only that there are some issues at the surface level that are frustrating the lives of ordinary people. Young conservatives, on the other hand, think that our civilisation is sick, festering with old tumours of which the cysts of transgenderism and critical race theory are mere symptoms — and for them it is precisely "ordinary people"

who are the problem, capitulating as they do at every stage
of our civilisation's self-destruction.

Boomer-cons still believe that the problems we face can be
solved by a moderate sense of patriotism, the freedom of the
market, and the procedures of old institutions. Young-cons
can't see how even moderate patriotism can be sustained in
a world of free movement, in which settled Western populations are routinely told that every culture is valuable except
their own; they don't see how the market can become the
benign force that boomers want it to be when it is led by
massive monopolising forces that possess colossal political
power, and which operate to destroy basic conservative sentiments; they can't grasp how the old institutions of state and
civil society can change the trajectory of civilisational decay
whilst such institutions are themselves the great engines taking us down this path to perdition. Young-cons may often
argue for the necessity of state intervention to protect civil
society, but the sort of state they have in mind is a radically
different one to that which governs us at present.

Where boomer-cons talk of free-speech, young-cons talk of
virtue. Where boomer-cons talk of national interest, young-
cons talk of the "common good." Where boomer-cons talk
of the primacy of the individual, young-cons talk of the
family and the need for cohesive tradition-based communities. Where boomer-cons talk of state intervention to protect freedom, young-cons talk of state coercion to promote
and protect human flourishing. Where boomer-cons talk
of "Judeo-Christian values," young-cons talk of conversion,
holiness, and Christendom.

Of course, there are millennial conservatives who look to
Thatcher and Reagan as the paradigmatic stars of conservatism, and there are boomer-aged conservatives who speak
with the purist blaze typical of the young-cons. A good
example of the latter is Peter Hitchens, who is routinely
mocked on mainstream media channels. But there are many
young-cons who aren't laughing. They hold Hitchens to be
someone who has seen perhaps better than anyone of his

generation that our problems are not superficial ones, but belong to a long and escalating spiritual crisis that's been engulfing the West for centuries. As Hitchens has put it, "I belonged to the last generation of Englishmen to see real England before it was finally destroyed altogether."

Many a time I have been in conversation with a boomer-con, agreeing with his observations on the woke indoctrination of young people in universities, the rise of pernicious activist movements, the absurdity of transgenderism, and so forth. Then, whenever a possible solution is proposed to such problems, the boomer will interject with, "Well yes, but of course, we must maintain a liberal approach to all that."

It is as if, in the boomer-con's mind, *liberalism* is a "nice principle" that ought to temper the "nasty but necessary principle" of conservatism. Young-cons, however, don't identify liberalism with niceness at all. They have suffered for decades the nastiness and antagonism of self-identified liberals. They've watched as so-called "liberal values" wrecked their parents' marriages, turned them into wage-slaves, isolated them from their neighbours, unanchored them from their civilisational inheritance, provided them with porn, emasculated them, encouraged them to treat others like objects of use, and told them to abort the offspring that they sired in the process. They've come out the other side of this nihilistic mayhem — with stories of terrible decisions from which they were never protected — covered in moral scars and often mortal scars. When they hear "liberalism" they don't think "nice," they think *evil*.

This is why, under the surface, at any given conservative conference or event, there is an unmistakeable division. Boomer-cons and young-cons nod along to each other's comments, but they know that were the conversation to continue for too long, that underlying division would emerge, exposed for all to see. Actually, one can never wholly hide it. These two groups necessarily look suspiciously at each other. When the boomer-con speaks, the young-con can hear

that his words are laced with liberal commitments that he
detests. When the young-con speaks, the boomer-con picks
up on the seeds of reactionism that he inevitably identifies
with fascism, and therefore fears that the intemperance of
the young-con will undermine the whole movement.

This, it seems to me, is the other problem that underpins
this generational divide among conservatives: boomer-con
discourse remains framed by the political and social concepts
initiated by the 20th century's first half. Boomer-cons still
think that the threats to the West are Marxism and fascism,
and that a liberal-conservative hybrid is what will protect
the West — and that this is in any case what we fought for
from 1939–45. They see transgenderism and attacks on free
speech as fundamentally Marxist, and they see the young-con
response to such phenomena as borderline fascist. Hence,
they have recourse to a theoretical liberal-conservative hybrid,
that now only lives on among them and in the smoking
rooms of Pall Mall clubs.

The boomer-cons fail to see that, whilst they're right that
*woke* is driven by Marxist theory, it is aided and abetted by
the most powerful institutions of State and society *because*
the materialism and nihilism of both Marxist and national
socialism won the ideological battle of the 20th century.
Socialism won, because the ideology that had the military
power (and later the financial power) to win out — namely
that very liberal-conservatism that boomers want to defend —
offered no coherent model for morally uniting the West in
the latter half of that century. Liberal-conservatism could do
little more than privatise the common goods of society and
re-establish public life on competitive goods, commodifying
all it touched. *That* was never going to provide the moral
vision to revive the West. Its competitors, then, won the
moral war. Hence, in the West we now suffer the statism,
thought-policing, and eugenic programmes of which Bol-
sheviks and Nazis could only have dreamed, and for good
measure we enjoy the class-tensions and race-conflicts which
were those ideologies' gifts to the world.

The political and cultural polemics of the first half of the 20th century are over, and it seems to me that this is what the boomer-con doesn't understand. The boomer-con still believes that an admixture of "conservative values" and "liberal approaches" is going to save the West from the fascistic "reactionary populists" on the Right and the Marxist, socialist woke mob on the Left. But the young-con is stood asking, "What West?" The West is gone. Its cities are crumbling, its political life is a meaning-vacuum steeped in petty and often contrived ideological aggression, its populations are rapidly disappearing and being replaced, and its national stories are derided. The vision of the post-war conservatives was insufficient to prevent this decay because they conceded so much to liberalism, and thus were left with little to say in the face of the socialist take-over — an admixture of both Marxist and national socialism — that has irreparably distorted their countries.

The worldview of the boomer-con continues to be informed by the project he embarked on of repairing the post-war, devastated world. The worldview of the young-con, however, is informed by the scars he carries in large part due to the failure of that project. The boomer was the last to see the final remnants of a tradition-based society, and because he encounters it occasionally in his London club or on a driven pheasant shoot, he thinks that that tradition-based society will always be there. The young-con, however, will likely never get a mortgage, let alone pay one off; he's terrified to begin a family because he has no money and he barely knows his own father, who left in a messy divorce when he was five; he knows that his society has disappeared and will radically change even in his lifetime; and he feels that he has no civilisation to pass on to his offspring for none was given to him. In fact, he knows of his civilisational tradition not because he was inducted into it by his family, his school, or his parish — quite the contrary — but because he occasionally encounters discussions of it in the comments sections of blog posts.

When the boomer-con and the young-con meet each other, they can't help but be suspicious of one another. They affirm each other's critical comments about transgenderism, critical race theory, cancel culture, and so on. But the boomer-con thinks that these are infections attacking an otherwise healthy organism. The young-con, however, thinks that the whole organism is failing, and that what the boomer diagnoses as infections are in fact *symptoms* of a far more serious disease that has taken over the whole body of Western civilisation. In order to treat this disease, according to the young-con, one has to do the hard work of studying the terrible diet, harmful habits, and deleterious lifestyle that this body has undergone for a long time, and then apply a very aggressive treatment in the hope of restoring health, and such a restoration is very far from certain. The boomer knows that this is what his younger equivalent really thinks, and he worries that this marks a return of fascism. Fascism, however, and all forms of noxious socialism, are precisely what the young-con can't stomach any longer.

Paradoxically, rather than liberalism bringing about the end of history, as the Fukuyaman adage has it, it brought about the end of modernity, largely by eating itself. Liberalism had no power to withstand the moral force of socialism. Now, the young-con holds, there is only one power that possesses the moral force to break the great socialist machine that operates as one device across the whole world: *Tradition.*

Between boomer-cons and young-cons there will ever be a distance, until the former give up on the dogmas of modernity altogether—and there's little chance of that. If young-cons keep to their convictions, the conservatism of future decades looks to be more realistic and aggressive, based on transcendent goods, a shared history, and a return of genuine culture. It will be a conservatism of the traditions of our civilisation, the traditions of Tradition if you like. In fact, the conservatism of the future may be something like a new Throne and Altar conservatism. Let's hope so.

## ⚜ 4 ⚜

# LIBERALISM'S PATHOLOGICAL AVERSION TO SUFFERING

ANY ERUDITE THINKERS HAVE written about how the age of social media and new virtual technologies are not so much placing us on the verge of a transhumanist world, but rather that we are already living in one. My friend Mary Harrington, for example, has pointed to the contraceptive pill as the first great transhumanist innovation, which she claims has moved us into a completely new paradigm with regard to what medicine and healthcare actually are, as well as how we relate to our very own bodies.[1] Harrington began as a feminist thinker, and today calls herself a "reactionary feminist," which has fast become a denotation for several public intellectuals who are developing certain feminist criticisms into a full-scale assault on late modernity. The contraceptive pill, Harrington argues, changed healthcare as a discipline exclusively ordered towards remedying failing bodies, to include the altering of well and properly functioning bodies as if they were problems to be solved. Whilst any contraception frustrates the procreative act, the pill is unique in doing this by chemically modifying what would otherwise be the natural functioning of the body. She claims that this explicitly moved us into the transhumanist epoch, in which we are now far more entrenched than we realise.

There are many ways, Harrington notes, in which we are already transhuman. The modern person conducts most of his relationships in a disembodied, technologically mediated way. He has, in many aspects of his life, adopted technologies

---

[1] See Mary Harrington, *Feminism Against Progress* (London: Forum, 2023).

not only as tools to be used but as teachers by which he may be formed and re-formed. Rather than developing opinions in order to live better, he doesn't really live, all the while habitually reacting to social media notifications about — you got it — how to live better. He fails to give his children the attention they need whilst he scrolls the comments sections of parenting websites. He delegates his own parenting to various screens left around the house. He no longer forms the habits of a sharp memory because he subcontracts his memory to his smart phone, which can recall for him any information he needs. He only moves in a world of objects out of necessity; his *real* self is an avatar that "interfaces" with other faceless avatars of the cyberworld, a "world" that now appears markedly more real to him than the domain of "medium-sized dry goods" (as the philosopher J. L. Austin called the world of our senses) that now seems a distant and uninteresting realm.

In a public talk delivered by Harrington which I attended some years ago, she quoted the historian and philosopher Yuval Harari, saying that "Modernity is essentially a pact that exchanges *meaning* for *power*." She traced this "pact" back to Bacon and Descartes, as is a common theme among historians of ideas. Downstream from their philosophical worldviews, she claimed, we have found ourselves jaded and "disenchanted" in late modernity, and thus we are currently witnessing in the "transhumanist revolution" a last desperate attempt to recover *meaning*. According to her, in this trans-humanist effort of technological encroachment, we are largely seeing a new form of Gnosticism emerging as a final pursuit of meaning, before the venture is snuffed out altogether by the impending paradigm of pure power. "Gnosticism" here chiefly means the radical conceptual separation of mind and body, the understanding of the "self" as a personal identity only accidentally related to the body, and the struggle to emancipate the self from embodied experience.

Harrington is undoubtedly right in her analysis of what we're witnessing in the near totally technologized era of late modernity, or what she calls "hyper-modernity." But I want to suggest—and Harrington agrees with me in this—that one of the problems associated with historians of ideas in general is that they see ideas as efficient causes of further ideas and more importantly of events, but they rarely see events as efficient causes of ideas. This, it seems to me, is a mistake. Indeed, I'm unconvinced that ideas possess the causal power that we tend to attribute to them—being as we are, inordinately conditioned by the truncated epistemology of rationalism.

It's no doubt true, for example, that the contractarianism with which Thomas Hobbes cursed the discipline of political philosophy enormously affected the world, and changed politics forever, and certainly for the worse. It is also no doubt true that Hobbes was deeply cognizant of the political tradition of Western Europe, and aware that his mind was deconstructing it like woodworm in an ancient church. Nonetheless, he desired to put an end to barbarism once and for all, to stamp out the bloodbathing of human history by subjugating the turbulent passions of the human hive to the "mortal god" of a draconian autarch. This universal servility, to which all would agree through a contract that raised man out of his natural atomised state and into the society of Leviathan, Hobbes envisaged would save man from himself. Such a view was not predominantly conjured up out of the world of ideas, but by the gore of the English Civil War, the astonishing violence of which—with brother slaying brother, and father slaying son—shook Hobbes to the core.

Take another example: It's no doubt true that the privatisation of religious or moral convictions which claim to follow from an objective apprehension of the good—a process of privatisation which is a chief characteristic of liberalism—came about by the convergence of certain ideas promulgated in the Anglosphere by the Lockean legacy, and on the Continent by that of Rousseau and the *philosophes*. But this privatisation of meaning also followed from the Peace of Westphalia's reduction of religious conviction to something arbitrarily determined by national borders, which was itself an event that was responding to ideas that had arisen from the *events* of the Thirty Years' War.

My point is that the genealogy of liberalism, which has morphed into progressivism, which itself is fast becoming transhumanist utopianism, is not merely one of a sequence of ideas in a causal chain. Rather, it is a genealogy of complex causal interplay of ideas and events. Those ideas and events are both stained with human suffering, from which arose the question of how to address the problem of human suffering, and ultimately how to *fix it*.

Transhumanism — and a particular development of transhumanism on which Harrington has especially focused, namely our approaching migration into the Metaverse — is certainly a new species of the ancient heresy of Gnosticism. But there is another aspect to this which I think at times has been neglected, one based less on the genealogy of ideas and more on the *experience* of suffering and liberalism's ongoing and ill-fated project to eliminate suffering.

John Locke, in his *Letter Concerning Toleration*, suggested that the law of the land ought to permit *all* religious practice and belief (except that of Catholic Christians) so long as such religious commitments didn't conflict with the law of the land in any way, because in his view politics was a public matter and religion a private matter. By so arguing, Locke was bringing to the fore the first principle of the liberal tradition. That principle is that all claims about the end for which we exist constitute private opinions, with which the state should be unconcerned. For Locke, the state should only be concerned with those moral requirements that maximise security and minimise suffering. Antithetical to the proposed Lockean political settlement would be any privileging of what we now call a "worldview" above any others, which would, according to Locke, invariably cause conflict and therefore suffering. (This, of course, is a self-defeating position, for the privatisation of worldviews is itself based on a worldview that claims to be universal, the disastrous effects of which we have had to watch unfold over the past three centuries.) This Lockean project marked the first big step towards ridding the public arena of all questions of *meaning* and *purpose*, leading to the very disenchanted, grey world that Harrington devastatingly diagnoses.

When I was growing up, it was widely said that there were three topics that should never be discussed: politics, sex, and religion. It's worth reflecting on this for a moment, for these three aspects of human life together cover the determinates of our existence. How we behave and live together in the building up of communities; how we form relationships, establish stable families, and produce offspring to which we can hand on our civilisation; and what the purpose of our being here actually *is* — these are the fundamental questions of human existence. The fact that English etiquette forbade anyone from discussing the purpose of our existence indicated to me that at some point in history a pathology had sunk its talons so deep into my nation's psyche that it had succeeded in never letting go. The corollary of this disdain for truth, one that we have exported to almost every corner of the world, is that we treat *niceness* — a "value" that rejects offending truths, which is to say, *all* truths — as the highest possible value. (Niceness, however, perpetuates the most horrific injustices, especially towards children, as is observable in the examples of divorce, abortion, and "transgender" mutilations, all of which are routinely defended on grounds of "niceness").

Liberalism as a political and social worldview adopted the paradigm bequeathed by Bacon and the 17th century "scientific revolution," which not only prioritised domination of nature over understanding of nature, but domination for the sake of human "progress." When firmly set within the framework of liberalism, this "progress" is largely understood as the ongoing process of privileging technique and technological advancement to eliminate suffering — suffering chiefly understood as *pain*. For this reason, those of us who are sceptical of the entire concept of "progress" as a theory of moral history — among whom Mary Harrington is a leading sceptic — are customarily told that we needn't look any further than the evolution of medical science to be convinced by this theory. This, of course, is because "moral progress" is understood by liberals principally to mean — perhaps *solely* to mean — the diminishment of suffering understood as pain. That's why the disappearance of beauty from our civilisation, and its replacement with mass production, junk art, and glassy, facetious architecture does not pose a problem to the liberal conception of "progress" — such things are simply outside the immediate concern of how to mitigate and hopefully eliminate pain. Moreover, the modern process of uglification's repudiation of antecedent forms indicates to the progressive that he is indeed leaving behind the world that has hitherto existed, with all its pain, and thus the marring of our world is something from which he can draw consolation.

One only needs to consider how we deal with death in our culture. Rather than the mature confrontation with death that characterised so much of the artistic inheritance of the West (and not the West only), we hide death, leaving people to perish alone in the cells of hospitals, or we whisk people away to be euthanised. Then, we refuse to look upon the dead body. Instead, we have it flame grilled to ash and thrown to the winds, that we might pretend that the deceased never really existed and thus nor did his death occur.

Today, one of the few ways in which we can maturely and ceremonially engage with the reality of suffering and death is through hunting, and hence it is an activity despised and derided by our liberal culture. The widespread disdain for hunting does not arise from a genuine concern for animal welfare, as most of those who condemn it will happily consume battery farmed chicken — whose death was no tragedy for the creature but a liberation from the wretched life of torture it had known since it hatched, already a mutant, in a dark metal container. In the end, the liberal, seeing that he cannot eliminate pain and death, will be content if they are hidden and he never has to think of them. Were a man to announce in polite company that he keeps rabbits not as pets but as food, and chooses to slaughter them himself, he would soon find oneself a pariah. The man who can maturely confront suffering and death, accepting them as undesirable yet unavoidable facts of life, is deemed a weirdo within the hypocritical liberal order.

Of course, the upshot of this pathological aversion to suffering is the absolute privileging of pleasure. And since certain pleasures are inextricably bound up with suffering, and other pleasures entail suffering if pursued to their excess, we end up with the sort of meaningless bio-asceticism which now characterises Western culture as a whole. It was precisely the absolute prioritising of pleasure, of appetitive stimulations and sensations, that led to the pornification of our culture, with the most extraordinary perversions immediately available for our voyeurism with just a few clicks on our ever-present portable devices. Now, we're porned-out, jaded, and exhausted. In turn, that suffering too must be eliminated, and the only way to do that is through liberation from the body itself.

The Metaverse, then, it seems to me, is the ultimate stage of liberalism's long history of eating itself. Having discovered that we can't eliminate all suffering, we have sought to hide it, and having hidden it we find it keeps sneaking out and finding us. A pandemic comes along and shakes us all up, and we think that we can stuff suffering back into its box and hide it away again if only the measures are severe enough and the hysteria excessive enough. What we cannot allow is the return of *pain*, for that would mean that liberalism's messianic enterprise really had failed.

We've tried to emancipate ourselves from every possible source of pain: we're now post-history, post-hierarchy, post-religion, post-metaphysics, and we're only a vaccine or two away from being post-suffering altogether . . . but the damn thing keeps coming back. Finally, now, we've found a way to deal with the suffering in our world once and for all: we shall flee this world altogether and enter a world of our own making, where there shall be no history, no future, no opinions, no pain, no suffering, no death, and the only value will be "niceness." Here, in the Metaverse, there will only be pleasure, and every pleasure will be cut loose from any correlated suffering. Behold, the end of the process of Progress.

It is inevitable that we, like all animals, should seek to minimise suffering and pursue pleasure. What liberalism has done, however, is take a natural impulse—and it is the fact that it is a natural impulse that accounts for liberalism's success—and turn it into a universal pathology. We must have the courage to say, in the words of John the Savage to Mustapha Mond in Huxley's *Brave New World*: "I'm claiming the right to be unhappy." The alternative is a grey and levelled world, one without meaning, without purpose, and submerged in a bubbling despair that will sooner or later blast like a faulty pressure cooker. And whilst I don't doubt that neo-Gnosticism is at the heart of how we found ourselves in the dismal condition in which we now toil, the pathological trepidation with which we approach pain must be a crucial part of the story. And it is time to write a new story, preferably one that tells the truth.

# 5

# CRIMINALISING "CONVERSION THERAPY" IN A LIBERAL DEMOCRACY

I N MAY OF 2022, PRINCE CHARLES, almost exactly one year before his coronation as King of the United Kingdom, for the first time opened Parliament. He was standing in for the Queen, who was suffering from poor health. He delivered the customary speech, conveying what Her Majesty expected of her government. Of course, the speech was written by the parliamentary ministers and simply listed what they had already decided upon. Thus, the entire event was—as it always is—theatre. It is important theatre, however, as it ceremonially reminds Parliament that it is not a self-serving oligarchy (or at least it shouldn't be) but a servant of the Crown and, by extension, of Her Majesty's subjects.

One of the Queen's orders was that legislation be "introduced to ban conversion therapy." I knew that this legislation was underway, but when I heard my future King say these words, it nonetheless came as a small shock to me.

Years ago, I listened to a lecture by the philosopher John Haldane during which he proposed the following thought experiment: imagine that a pharmaceutical company created a medically safe drug that, when taken, caused those with same-sex attraction to experience sexual attraction only towards members of the other sex. In short, imagine that a company invented a drug that would turn homosexuals into heterosexuals. Then Haldane asked: "Would Western governments outlaw such a drug?"

The question that Haldane was really asking—in his own brilliant, Socratic way—was: are "liberal democracies" what they claim to be? We are told that we live in a liberal democracy. Indeed, early on, the Queen's speech delivered by the then Prince Charles had explicitly stated that the UK government must "play a leading role in defending freedom and democracy across the world." Clearly, Westminster powerholders see themselves as exemplars in the cause for liberal democracy.

"Liberal democracy" does not so much denote a governmental *form*, but a moral stance presupposed by modern democratic governments (which can themselves take different constitutional forms in different countries). What is this moral stance? In short, it is the view that politics should protect the liberties and dispense the rights necessary for the individual to pursue his self-realisation according to his own lights (insofar as such a pursuit does not excessively interfere with others' pursuits of self-realisation according to their own lights). Liberal democracy, then, claims to have no moral dogmas of its own beyond that of the sovereignty of the individual. The job of liberal democracy, its advocates claim, is merely to expand and protect conditions needed for the self-determining, sovereign individual to undertake his journey of self-realisation.

With this new legislation to outlaw "conversion therapy," I think we now know the answer to the question raised by Haldane's thought experiment.

Imagine the following case. A man in his late twenties is sexually attracted only to other men. This, however, is a problem for what he deems his own journey of self-realisation. Why? Because he equates marrying a woman, and having children with her, with his own personal flourishing. He is unhappy that his sexual impulses appear incompatible with the life he wants to live. Given that those of the LGBTQ+ community, of which he is unwillingly a member, can legally undergo major invasive surgery in pursuit of self-realisation, why cannot he, he asks himself, have recourse to therapeutic assistance to pursue *his* own personal self-realisation? So, he goes to a psychotherapist and presents his conundrum.

To this, the therapist replies: "Well, we can certainly spend time discussing your life-history, giving attention to key moments that might help you understand your same-sex attraction. Given the general complexity of human sexuality, it is possible that our sessions could bring about a change in sexual attraction, perhaps away from men and towards women. If you like, as we talk, I can keep in mind that this change is what you want."

At the time of writing, there are plans afoot to make such a response in the context of professional therapeutic care a criminal offence in the UK. There are many countries throughout the world where this is already the case. Note that the imagined therapist's response above does not indicate any kind of moral judgement on homosexuality. In fact, the therapist would be consistent in responding this way due in part to a commitment to *liberal democracy*. In turn, the question arises: do we even live in a liberal democracy?

What perhaps we *really* inhabit is a political and social system which presupposes that reductionist materialism is true. Modern societies certainly seem largely to operate on the assumption that all human desires can be satisfied by the satiating of appetite and the accumulation of commodities. Modern man is seen first and foremost to be a *consumer*.

How is it, we may reasonably ask ourselves, that sexuality is widely deemed something fluid, unless its fluidity runs towards heterosexuality, and then all of a sudden sexuality becomes a binary phenomenon that cannot undergo any change ("born that way," as the oft-repeated phrase goes)? Perhaps, it is because there is something about the homosexual that is preferable to the heterosexual once man is framed as *homo consumericus*.

In many ways, the man whose income is his own, who can live and work anywhere, whose sexual pursuits need not change that, and whose desire for fatherhood can be satisfied by the surrogacy trade (that is, by the market), is the perfect citizen for our modern settlement of insulated producer-consumers. Conversely, the married, settled, child-begetting man will necessarily have a set of commitments that transcend appetitive pleasure and what the market can deliver. If this is correct, in the political and social framework based on the primacy of pleasure and commodity-accumulation, legislation and culture will naturally privilege homosexuality. In short, the homosexual is the ideal member of our decadent, capitalist anti-culture.

In turn, "liberal democracy" seems to be a euphemism for reductionist materialism transposed into political life. And reductionist materialism definitely *does* have moral dogmas. The 51% of people in England and Wales who identify as Christian enjoy almost no public celebration — and frequent denigration — of their religion in their constitutionally Christian country. And yet months of public celebration, with rainbow flags everywhere, and massive, publicly funded parades to boot, is patiently endured by everyone for the sake of a whopping 2.7% of the population.

At the level of our political class, there seems to be a moral preference for one of those groups over the other. Those who claim to advance liberal democracy — that worldview that has no moral dogmas beyond the sovereignty of the individual — are not honest. In fact, they have a strongly held code of moral dogmas based on reductionist materialism, and they are pleased to deploy directive and coercive means to promote them.

As it happens, I don't think the solution to the problem I have presented above is that of realising a *true* liberal democracy. I don't mind the State being committed to moral dogmas, and even curtailing the self-determination of citizens in the light of those dogmas. I don't even mind if the State's moral dogmas are in some ways erroneous, if not gravely so, as I hardly expect politics to always get things right. What I despise, however, is the State coercing its citizens on ideological grounds whilst claiming not to do so. What we have, at present, is *dishonesty by establishment*. If the State is going to coerce its citizens on the grounds of exceedingly dubious moral dogmas, it could at least be honest about it.

## 6

# MIDWITS

## THE TRUE ENEMIES OF COUNTER-REVOLUTION

N HIS POEM PUBLISHED IN 1711, *AN Essay on Criticism*, Alexander Pope masterly presented an issue that has come to be known in our day as the "problem of the midwit":

> A little learning is a dang'rous thing;
> Drink deep, or taste not the Pierian spring:
> There shallow draughts intoxicate the brain,
> And drinking largely sobers us again.

Some years ago, internet reactionaries discovered the truth contained in Pope's poem when they discerned that, whilst their opponents were not unclever, nor were they very clever; they were "midwits." As is now customary, this observation soon became an internet "meme." And like so many memes, its content was not a mere joke. Indeed, according to William M. Briggs, once a professor at Cornell University, there is a "deep truth in the Midwit Meme."[1]

On the *spectrum* of general education and aptitude for insight and understanding, at one end there are those who are educated at the "university of life" or the "school of hard knocks," as they say. These people can and often do enjoy quite acute insight and understanding of the world, but it is almost wholly implicitly, with little ability to convey their understanding with any complexity or dexterity. Then there are those at the other end of that spectrum; these have undertaken extremely rigorous educations, not only

---

[1] See William M. Briggs, *The Deep Truth in The Midwit Meme*, https://www.wmbriggs.com/post/32221/

through specialisation but via a truly wide-ranging, humane formation. Such formation provides both breadth and depth of knowledge, allowing its beneficiaries to enjoy profound understanding as well as the ability to communicate with precision their premises, logic, and conclusions, and often anticipate counterarguments to boot.

The Midwit Meme claims that these two groups, at either end of the spectrum, largely agree with one another on most fundamentals. The uneducated and the very educated are, the meme claims, natural allies. The real problem is found with those towards the centre of the spectrum, the *slightly educated* lot. As Briggs notes, it is here that you find bureaucrats, politicians, propagandists — "those with college degrees and professorships." It is also the home of those who say "ackchyually," those who raise the pitch of their voices at the end of propositions so they sound like patronising rhetorical questions, and the "I f****ing LOVE science!" crowd.

Before I was introduced to the term "midwit" and its meme, I came across the idea in an interview with the evolutionary biologist Bret Weinstein. During the interview, Weinstein illustrated the problem of midwittery with the example of what would happen if you were to ask different people the same question, namely, "Are whales fish?" When asked, a person with a substandard education will generally say *yes*, since he supposes that a fish is an animal with fins that lives in water, and therefore a whale must be a fish. On asking the same question to a highly educated person, who analyses the question carefully, generally he will also respond with *yes*, since he judges that the term "fish" is a loose category for animals that share a certain living condition, namely they live an aquatic life. (Thus, scaled fish, unscaled fish, non-skeletal animals like jellyfish, and exoskeletal creatures like shellfish are all justly called fish.) Weinstein explained that only the standard university graduate, the *slightly educated* person, will tend to answer with "No, they are mammals." Whilst believing himself to be demonstrating his learning, he in fact mistakenly judges "fish" to denote a genus of animals, rather than a reference to a condition shared by many genera and species. The uneducated person, relying chiefly upon uncriticised assumptions and intuition, and the educated person, possessing enough learning to approach the question cautiously and humbly, arrive at the same conclusion. The *slightly educated* person, knowing little but having great confidence in his limited learning, gets it wrong.

Interestingly, long before the rise of the Midwit Meme, counter-revolutionary thinkers Edmund Burke and Joseph de Maistre made similar observations.

In *Reflections on the Revolution in France*, Burke criticises at length those who are not guided by "respect for the wisdom of others" but also not by "prejudice" and unexamined "habit," but rather approach complex problems "with no better apparatus than the metaphysics of an undergraduate."[2]

Burke believed that the mechanistic politics that the half-educated rationalists of his age were advancing would give rise to a social settlement increasingly run, not by true statesmen, but by a class of technocratic managers. This suspicion is voiced in his concern that a democratised age would eventually bring about "a mischievous and ignoble oligarchy" with a purely "geometrical and arithmetical" conception of society.[3] In opposition to the assumption that favours quickly acquired elite technical knowledge over socially developed experience and prudence, Burke wrote the following:

> Though you were to join in the commission all the directors of the two academies to the directors of the Caisse d'Escompte [revolutionary France's central bank], one old experienced peasant is worth them all. I have got more information, upon a curious and interesting branch of husbandry, in one short conversation with a Carthusian monk, than I have derived from all the bank directors that I have ever conversed with.[4]

---

[2] Burke, *Reflections*, 183–184, 299.
[3] Ibid., 228, 144.
[4] Ibid., 309.

Here, Burke makes his view clear: the world does not need more "experts." The world needs people immersed in a culture, who are neighbours to each other, full of *real* learning — whether learning that comes by worldly experience or by slow and humble formation in the Great Tradition.

I have always been suspicious of the title "expert," indeed as much as "intellectual." These terms have a gnostic character to them, as if having one of these denotations predicated of you raises you to a special class of *perfecti*, suspended over the rest of society. These terms connote something very different to the truly "educated person" or to the "gentleman" of John Henry Newman's *The Idea of a University*.[5] Newman — a typical Burkean — presented the *gentleman* as someone who does not stand over society whilst never truly belonging to it. Rather, he is educated *for* society. The Newmanian gentleman seeks in education the transformation of himself as a whole and integrated person, so as to make the most generous contribution he can to his fellow countrymen, with whom he stands shoulder to shoulder in the public square. What is perhaps most interesting about the midwit is that he sees himself as an intellectual standing in a position of judgement.

Maistre highlights the problem of the midwit in *The Saint Petersburg Dialogues*. In an interesting philological discussion, Maistre notes that language is not imposed by a particular section of any given society, but a prerequisite for belonging to that society, ever shaping its culture and historical direction.[6] Maistre holds that there is something deeply mysterious about language: the conveying of intelligible truth — the ideas in the human mind — by the spoken word, bringing forth truth into time. Indeed, for Maistre, all human language is a fragmented possession of the perfect,

---

[5] See John Henry Newman, *The Idea of a University* ([n.p.] Assumption Press, 2014), 163.
[6] See Joseph de Maistre, 'The Saint Petersburg Dialogues' in *The Generative Principle of Political Constitutions: Studies on Sovereignty, Religion, and Enlightenment*, edited by Jack Lively (Abingdon: Routledge, 2017), 205–210.

unified language which is the Word in the triune life of God. Every distinct language is, then, a national possession of the Eternal Logos. All who possess something of language have made their own a portion of the wisdom of God.

Maistre despised the view of the philosopher Étienne Bonnot de Condillac that most social problems could be remedied by subjecting all language to philosophic correction (a notion reintroduced by some analytic philosophers in the 20th century). Condillac was essentially transposing Enlightenment assumptions in political thought to the realm of language, namely that "Reason," independent of context, history, shared cultural commitments, and so forth, could purify and bring to perfection something historically conditioned, contextual, and particular. In opposition to this view, Maistre asserted that "language could not be created *a priori* or perfected by the wit of man or philosopher."[7] Maistre trusted the language of the ordinary man and rejected the idea that only language purified by a "rational" class, who could philosophically scrutinise and cleanse it, was true language.

Maistre, contrary to Condillac, argued that it is precisely because of the common and unexamined nature of language, that the moral intuitions of the uneducated are largely to be trusted. The uneducated person's unexamined language expresses moral prejudices and uncriticised assumptions which, Maistre argues, are generally trustworthy, for such prejudices and assumptions comprise the general moral deposit that has shaped a cohesive society.[8] So too, the truly and profoundly educated person is someone who has learned enough to know that his knowledge is in fact very limited, and hugely dependent on the knowledge of others, and therefore he is also generally to be trusted.

The dangerous person, for Maistre, is the person situated between these two: the *slightly educated* person — or, if you like, the *midwit*. This person has learned enough to convince himself that he knows something, but not enough to see

---

[7] Ibid., 15.
[8] See Joseph de Maistre, *The Pope*, xvii–xviii.

that this something is very little, and part of a larger context. Such a person, with a very truncated conception of the span of reality, is quickly driven to stand in judgement over his society, which he does not understand, but believes himself to have comprehended in its entirety. The slightly educated person believes that he knows reality, and therefore that he can judge it. He does not, however, really know much at all. This is what Maistre means by his relentless criticisms of "individual reason." The slightly educated person understands little besides his *ideas* about the reality which he does not well understand. He does not return from those ideas back to the reality of which they are abstractions, abstractions to which he anxiously and unsuccessfully seeks to conform the world. The slightly educated person, in other words, is a natural rationalist, prone to unite himself to revolutionary causes.

In Maistre's view, the uneducated person and the truly educated person see themselves as members of the same community; the *slightly educated* person sees himself as belonging to what Maistre sarcastically calls "the Elect." As Enlightenment scholar Jack Lively presents Maistre's position: "it was not the Elect who could hear this inner voice of conscience, but the unsophisticated, all those unstained by excessive rationalism — and this was a state within all man's capacities."[9]

It is noteworthy, then, that in conservative and reactionary circles, the problem of the midwit has emerged as a major theme for classifying those who would have little or no sympathy for traditionalist arguments and objections. By identifying the epistemic problem of midwittery, these online reactionaries stand in a long tradition of counter-revolutionary thinkers going back to those two great men, Burke and Maistre, who exhausted themselves attempting to slam the brakes on the French Revolution and its poisonous fruit, the Terror.

---

[9] Jack Lively, in Maistre, *The Generative Principle*, 18.

## ⚜ 7 ⚜

# SHOULD WE CALL
# OURSELVES CONSERVATIVES?

N OCTOBER OF 2022, A CALL TO ARMS—
metaphorically speaking—was issued in a piece published
by *The Federalist*, written by one of its senior editors, the
journalist John Daniel Davidson, entitled "We Need To Stop
Calling Ourselves Conservatives."[1] This piece was shared
widely on social media and received much praise from the
internet Right, and rightly so. I found little in the piece with
which to disagree, and much to affirm. Nonetheless, in its
light, I want to offer a defence of the word "conservative,"
which he argues we should renounce, and I want to explain
why I think the term may still have some utility.

Davidson begins with a list of how conservatives have
failed to conserve much at all, and he remarks on how they
have effectively lost the culture war. I don't disagree, but
when one considers the ambitions of post-war liberals, progressives, socialists, and communists, who knows what the
world would have looked like now had it not been for the
relentless challenges launched by old fashioned "paleo" conservatives over the decades to slow the process of cultural
revolution?

In any case, it does not follow from taking stock in the
way that Davidson does that the conservative cause needs to
be abandoned, or the name of that cause discarded. Spain,
century after century, was conquered by a north African
force that despised Christendom, whose glories had been
so visible in Spain in particular. Eventually, all Iberia was
conquered but for the little kingdom of Castille. From there,

---

[1] John Daniel Davidson, *We Need To Stop Calling Ourselves Conservatives*, https://thefederalist.com/2022/10/20/we-need-to-stop-calling-
ourselves-conservatives/

however, the *Reconquista* began, eventually taking back the whole peninsula. Acknowledging failure can lead to action.

Of course conservatives should, as Davidson calls them to do, consider their unhappy situation. The ideology of progressivism that now dominates the West, which seeks to repudiate our civilisation and replace our shared life based on the common good with the chaos of competing appetites of isolated individuals, has conquered our nations and their noblest institutions. As Davidson says, conservatives must stop fantasising about 1980s-style market-based politics or libertarian small government settlements. They must, instead, instigate a *Reconquista*.

The argument from which Davidson derives the title of his piece seems one to which he himself is not committed. At one point Davidson says that conservatives need to stop calling themselves by that name and "start thinking of themselves as radicals, restorationists, and counterrevolutionaries." He, however, does not adopt any of those denotations for the rest of his piece, remaining content to call conservatives *conservatives*. Perhaps this is because he sees that conservatism is already — quite organically — adopting the approaches to cultural, moral, and political discourse that terms like "radical," "restorationist," and "counterrevolutionary" connote.

Take the word "radical." This word, as many know, etymologically means *to return to the roots*. Conservatives in the 1980s and '90s — apart from a few eccentrics like Russell Kirk and Roger Scruton, at whom the Reaganites and Thatcherites always looked sideways — were not reading Edmund Burke. Well, conservatives today are reading him. In fact, they are reading many of those who led the counter-Enlightenment movement whence we get the word "conservative": Burke, Maistre, Bonald, Chateaubriand, Donoso, Coleridge, Cobbett, Newman, Chesterton, Eliot, Kirk, Scruton, and so on. They are also reading Plato, Aristotle, Cicero, Seneca, Boethius, Augustine, and Aquinas. Having taken stock and acknowledged the colossal failure of conservatism to which

Davidson refers at the beginning of his piece, young conservatives especially are going back to the *roots*, discovering the principles of their political and social tradition, and those who applied them in defence of their civilisation.

This is how "counterrevolution" and "restoration" begin. Returning to our roots in order to equip ourselves against revolution, for the sake of restoring what has been taken from us, is exactly what conservatism is all about — or what it should be about. And the word *conservatism* itself is significant because it indicates that conservatives are not simply protesting against something. The conservative creed is not a negative creed, and in this way conservatives are wholly different to their political, moral, and cultural adversaries who know of nothing but the impulse to repudiate. Conservatives are meant to *affirm* something, to affirm their civilisation and how to *conserve* it. As Scruton used to say, conservatism is — at the most fundamental level — about love.

The word "conservatism" is important because, as I have indicated, it is bound up with a canon of thought. And that canon is one with which conservatives should continue to familiarise themselves if they are going to recapture what they deem rightfully theirs, namely their civilisational inheritance. People on the Right who stray from that canon are routinely seduced by the unhinged esotericism of a Julius Evola or a Savitri Devi Mukherji, or the vast store of cod-Nietzschean neo-paganism out there in the blogosphere, whose material would be hilarious if it were not so corrupting of its young readership.

Unforeseen dangers lurk, and it is plausible that they will reveal themselves too late for us to do anything about them if conservatives abandon the term "conservative." Names are important, and the name "conservative" is important if conservatives are not to forget who they are and what they strive for.

A major theme of Davidson's piece concerns the threat of new technologies, to which narrower "culture war" issues remain secondary in his opinion. He believes that

conservatism, or what it denotes, is unfit to address the
dangers posed by such technologies. Again, I do not entirely
dissent, but new technologies always shake the settled life
of established societies. When the new technology of the
printing press emerged, it was initially used to break up
the religious unity of Christendom; thereafter, however, it
became a major force for cultural and religious cohesion.

Social media and computer technology has been, no doubt,
a colossal force for evil in the world, and has contributed in
untold ways to the mass surveillance under which we all now
toil. There are many ways in which new digital technologies
have been and continue to be corrupting of our nature.
Nonetheless, it is necessary to acknowledge that they have
also made the finest books ever written instantly available
to everyone, and thus made it possible for a low-wage earner
to have a library at his fingertips that Samuel Johnson could
only have dreamed of. To treat new technologies as if they
couldn't, with help from the coercive apparatus of a just
and well-functioning State, be assumed by a conservative
social order for the flourishing of its members is, I think,
to underestimate its potential for the good.

I often place a particular quotation from Newman in
my writing, because I think it is both the best and pithiest
summary of the conservative cause I have ever read: conservatism, Newman tells us, is about finding "some way of
uniting what is free in the new structure of society with
what is authoritative in the old, without any base com-
promise with 'progress' and 'liberalism.'"[2] The challenge
before us is that of uniting the new technologies of the day
with the moral law that has had authority over us throughout the course of our civilisation until our accursed age.
Most philosophical classics, patristic works, and the whole
*Summa Theologiae* can be found on the internet, but so
can the most abominable perversions known to man. A
conservative social order would keep the former and ban

---

[2] Newman, *A Letter Addressed to the Duke of Norfolk*, 54–55.

access to the latter, and thereby unite what is free in the *new* with what was authoritative in the *old*. Basically, under a just government, the citizenry would consume less porn and more Aquinas.

Davidson proceeds to say that conservatives should want to be "wielding government power," and that this "will mean a dramatic expansion of the criminal code." Perhaps this is true, but conservatives have never believed that social transformation for the sake of the common good is exclusively obtained by coercion, even if law and its enforcement are a major component. Conservatives have always held that for the felicity of society — that it may not descend into political collapse (which is only ever a few bad decisions away) — *interior transformation* is required, namely *virtue*. Law does of course have a didactic dimension, but this aspect can only be expected to have the desired effect when it is supported by a broader culture that prizes virtue. The fact, then, that conservatism is observably becoming an increasingly religious social force is encouraging.

Interior transformation by the cultivation of virtue is growing into a major topic again in conservative thought. It is striking that, contrary to what people predicted only a few decades ago, conservatism — especially among young people on the Right — is not redefining itself as a secular cause for Western values. Rather, it is becoming a deeply reactionary cause that is both aggressively political and profoundly religious.

Whether one looks at the NatCon guys or PostLibs on Davidson's side of the Atlantic, or the Vanenburg or Radical Orthodoxy lot on this side, terms like "Christendom," "Integralism," and "religious identity" have been on everyone's lips recently. Conservatives are rediscovering the need for public religion — *true* public religion — to bring about the civic virtue that is the prerequisite for conserving civilisation (which, after all, is the proper cause of conservatism). Davidson seems to recognise this phenomenon when he writes that to "talk of defending 'religious freedom' is to misapprehend that the real risk today is widespread irreligion." In his concern here, however, he ought to feel at home with the conservatism that is rapidly becoming the mainstream of the Right.

Davidson says that conservatives need to give up their attachment to "small government" and embrace political power to achieve their objectives. This strikes one as an attack on a straw man. True conservatives have never said otherwise and have always recognised the need for a robust, healthy State. What conservatives *have* insisted upon, traditionally, is that such a State need not be excessively centralised or unnecessarily intrusive on the lives of the citizenry, and that the best way to have a vigorous State that resists totalitarian tendencies is to arrange political power subsidiarily.

Sound-thinking conservatives, who have always believed that the market's freedom must be balanced by paternalism for the sake of the common good, would readily agree with Davidson's following recommendations for how political power might be used:

> To stop Big Tech, for example, will require using antitrust powers to break up the largest Silicon Valley firms. To stop universities from spreading poisonous ideologies will require state legislatures to starve them of public funds. To stop the dis-integration of the family might require reversing the travesty of no-fault divorce, combined with generous subsidies for families with small children. Conservatives need not shy away from making these arguments because they betray some cher-ished libertarian fantasy about free markets and small government.

Indeed, as he says, conservatives need not shy away from such arguments. If conservatives were more familiar with their own political and moral tradition, they would not shy away from these arguments but see them for what they are: conservative arguments. And conservatives need not disavow their own name of "conservative" in order to embrace such arguments, but rather must reaffirm that to be conservative is to champion the cause of the common good—by direct political intervention if necessary.

Conservatives are now faced with a unique opportunity. Liberalism has made people miserable. The isolated individual pursuing his own appetitive impulses is a deeply unhappy person. The suicide rate in the West is a clear indication of this fact. In the UK alone, suicide is a leading cause of death, especially among men. The emancipation and personal flourishing promised by liberalism never arrived. By equating human flourishing with production and consumption, and thus levelling everything to the level of commodification, liberalism locked us up in our own selfish appetites, creating an epoch of chronic loneliness and misery.

This moment is a very special opportunity that conservatives would be foolish to miss. Perhaps in decades past, the conservative cause looked like an attempt to direct people back into a cage at the very moment they felt themselves emancipated. Now, however, people are crying out to be liberated from the fetters of self-indulgence and reclaim their "roots." They want to engage in a "meaning-based" discourse, and it is in such a discourse that the conservative tradition can shine like a great beacon leading people into the calm harbour of sanity. This, then, is an important moment for a true conservative revival, but conservatives—calling themselves *conservatives*—will need to wake up and seize it.

## PART IV

# BREAKING FREE
# BY BINDING
# OURSELVES

# TOWARDS A
# RIGHT-WING ECUMENISM

## BURKE, MAISTRE, AND SOLOVYOV

WHEN "ECUMENISM" IS BANDIED around in today's churchy circles, it invariably denotes a progressivist agenda of denying or downplaying differences of moral and doctrinal conviction among different kinds of Christians, for the sake of a sort of bourgeois ecclesiastical etiquette. That Christians—by which I simply mean baptised people—of different denominations and ecclesial communities have drastically different views on everything from the nature (or rather, natures) of the Incarnation to which bedroom behaviours are prohibited by the moral law remains undiscussed for the sake of *ecumenism*.

The oft-expressed impatience with such indifference to truth among more conservative or traditional Christians is due to the view, which is right in my opinion, that ecumenism perpetuates division among Christians by pretending that such division is unimportant. Rather, traditional Christians claim, it is better to address and discuss religious divisions, with a view to condemning error and returning the separated brethren to the fold. Who exactly the separated ones are depends on which camp you're in.

As I say, I sympathise with this general animosity towards the ecumenical project, a project that has been so fashionable throughout the latter half of the 20th century. After all, I opted out of the Anglican Communion and became a Roman Catholic a decade and a half ago precisely because I thought, and continue to think, that religious claims and their veracity matter.

Judging the merits of ecumenism, however, is not straight-forward. I worked as an official of an Archdiocese for many years, training people for ministry in the Catholic Church, and part of my role was the agonisingly penitential task of going to diocesan and national church conferences. Time and again, I had the experience of being surrounded by my Catholic coreligionists and seeing that my beliefs and theirs had little to do with one another. This is, of course, because the Catholic Church is largely run by progressivist activists who are deeply embarrassed by the Church's tradition and doctrine.

One can, then, it seems to me, be in canonical unity with another person, and be in both doctrinal and spiritual disunity with him. So too, however, perhaps one can be in canoni-cal and doctrinal disunity with someone and be in spiritual unity with him — this is something I have experienced with many Evangelicals, in fact. The Italian philosopher Augusto del Noce remarked that "a progressive Catholic is closer to a non-Catholic progressive than to a non-progressive Catholic." This is no doubt true, but conversely a conservative Catholic is closer to a non-Catholic conservative than to a progressive Catholic. I know Anglicans who are pious, devout, pro-life, pro-family, patriotic, and disciplined. I also know Catholics who consider the devotional life folly, are antinatalist, globalist, and "woke." Of these, I know whom I deem my allies.

I want, then, to propose a *right-wing ecumenism*. I want to suggest that the members of the baptised, whatever their religious divisions, work together to undermine and ulti-mately destroy the progressivist supremacy that dominates the West, recognising that it marks a settlement incompatible with even a basic Biblical worldview. Such an ecumenism need not be born from indifference to moral and theological differences, but rather based on a prudential acknowledgment that such division must be worked out in friendship whilst Christians face their common enemy.

The rising technocratic utopianism that is foundered on the replacement of God and His providential care for man-kind with the technical expertise of a mischievous oligarchy will likely soon replace its mockery of Christians with outright persecution — in fact, this has already begun. The baptised are better together, and since their visible ecclesiastical institutions have been colonised by their enemies, they're going to have to fall back on something other than denominational identity — so let it be their shared love for Jesus Christ.

Edmund Burke, in the face of the French Revolution, and the very real possibility of such a Jacobin-led revolution making its way across the Channel, emphasised the commonly held beliefs of Catholics and Anglicans. He argued for Catholic Emancipation, political representation for Catholics (especially in Ireland), and encouraged the offering of refuge to Catholic clergy escaping the Terror. He suggested that Anglicans should not consider themselves Protestants against Catholicism, and he advocated an early "branch theory" of ecclesiology, declaring that "a man is certainly the most perfect Protestant who protests against the whole Christian religion."[1] Those fellow Whigs who continued to harbour anti-Catholic sentiments he called, in *The Reflections*, "miserable bigots."[2] For Burke, as the great revolt against Christendom exploded, it was the unity of the baptised that had to be emphasised and fostered.

Joseph de Maistre, for his part, despite locating the origins of the French Revolution in the Protestant revolt of the 16th century, called for a counter-revolutionary ecumenism. In fact, he believed that the Anglican Church may be ideally placed as a sort of bridge between the Roman Catholic Church and all the fragmented Protestant sects that had emerged since the time of Luther. It was Maistre's hope that the Church of England would eventually reunite with Rome and bring many Protestant groups with it. Maistre discerned the work of providence in the Revolution's driving of Catholic clergy out of France. "It was probably necessary that French priests be

---

[1]  Edmund Burke, *A Letter to Sir Hercules Langrishe, On the Subject of the Roman Catholics of Ireland*, http://www.ricorso.net/rx/library/authors/classic/Burke_E/Works_1887/Langrishe_1792.htm

[2]  Burke, *Reflections*, 257.

displayed to foreign nations," he wrote in the *Considerations*, "they have lived among Protestant peoples, and this coming together has greatly diminished hatreds and prejudices."[3] Maistre then proceeded to imagine meetings of Catholics and Anglicans, and expressed his longing for Christian unity:

> The considerable emigration of clergy, especially French bishops, to England, appears to me a particularly remarkable event. Surely, words of peace will have been spoken and projects for reconciliation formed during this extraordinary meeting. Even if mutual hopes are all that result, this would be a lot. If ever Christians are to be reconciled, and everything suggests that they should, it seems that the *initiative* must come from the Church of England.[4]

It is difficult not to laugh at the notion of an Anglican-led right-wing ecumenism, given that the Anglican hierarchy is such an infernal basket case. On the other hand, just look at the Catholic hierarchy! The fact is that all ecclesiastical institutions have been radically colonised by progressivist ideologues, which is why any future salvaging of our civilisation may unavoidably be the task of the lay faithful.

The philosopher and theologian Vladimir Solovyov, in his *The Antichrist*, portrays what he imagines as a future usurpation — taking place in the 21st century — of the visible institution of the Church by globalist and utopian powers led by the Antichrist. In a striking passage, the Antichrist compares his "values" to the salvific imperatives of Jesus Christ:

> I am called to be the benefactor of . . . humanity, partly reformed and partly incapable of being reformed. I will give everyone what they require. As a moralist, Christ divided humanity by the notion of good and evil. I shall unite it by benefits which are as much needed by good as by evil people. I shall be the true representative of that God who makes his sun to shine upon the good

---

[3] Maistre, *Considerations*, 19.
[4] Ibid., 19.

and the evil alike, and who makes the rain to fall upon the just and the unjust. Christ brought the sword; I shall bring peace. Christ threatened the earth with the Day of Judgment. But I shall be the last judge, and my judgment will be not only that of justice but also that of mercy. The justice that will be meted out in my sentences will not be a retributive justice but a distributive one. I shall judge each person according to his deserts, and shall give everybody what he needs.[5]

The Antichrist is thus the embodiment of "Enlightenment values." For him, the moral good is a private matter for each individual. The only thing that really matters, publicly that is, is the proper distribution of competitive goods — and yet it is *he* who holds all the power. Solovyov's Antichrist might have used the infamous phrase of the World Economic Forum to convey just the same thing: "You will own nothing, and you will be happy."

The Antichrist is, in Solovyov's account, the personification of liberalism and progressivism. In a terrific triumph of rationalism, the Antichrist publishes a book, *The Open Path to World Peace and Welfare*, a technical manual whose principles will lead to the utopia that we've all been promised since the Enlightenment. As the theologian Hans Urs von Balthasar commented, the Antichrist's book offers "an all-embracing programme that unites all contradictions in itself — the highest degree of freedom of thought and a comprehension of every mystical system, unrestricted individualism and a glowing devotion to the general good." The Antichrist's tome is applauded everywhere. He is soon elected the "Emperor of the United States of Europe," with the support of the vast majority of Christians. Finally, his authority is recognised across all nations, and he forms a single world government.

For all the Antichrist's claims that he is bringing peace where Christ brought a sword, he in fact brings a sword of

---

[5] Vladimir Solovyov, *The Antichrist* (Edinburgh: Floris Books, 1982), 25.

his own. His very ascendency divides the baptised between genuine Christian disciples and lukewarm adherents of an unchallenging religion. Catholic, Orthodox, and Protestant Christians who had privileged temporal concerns and tacitly given up on grace, ecumenically unite under the leadership of the Emperor. He hasn't taken away Christianity, they say, but given it to us again only without the Cross — it is better than before. To steal a line from Aldous Huxley, the Emperor gives to the world "Christianity without tears."

But so too Catholic, Orthodox, and Protestant Christians who had sought to remain faithful to the Gospel develop their own ecumenism under the leadership of three figures: Pope Peter II, the Russian eremitical monk John the Elder, and the Lutheran biblical scholar Professor Ernst Pauli. They don't believe in a universal benevolence towards humanity, but in the hard work of loving one's neighbour — a love of which they think man incapable outside the path of grace and suffering. Together, this remnant of genuine disciples stands alone in the world, opposing the Emperor, and are unanimously condemned as haters and trouble-makers.

In Solovyov's story, the Pope's Petrine authority is recognised by John the Elder (who represents the Johannine charism of the "beloved disciple") and Professor Pauli (representing the didactic Pauline charism), and together they enter the Roman fold — just as Solovyov himself eventually did. Real ecumenism achieves its finality at the eschaton, as the true disciples become one Church.

I won't ruin it for those who have yet to read Solovyov's *The Antichrist* by describing the glorious culmination of events following this ecclesial reconciliation. The point I wish only to highlight is that Maistre, Solovyov, and Burke — a Catholic, an Orthodox, and a Protestant — all saw the need to develop (for want of a better term) a "counter-revolutionary ecumenism" in the face of the rationalist and progressivist takeover that *is* modernity. In this, as in so much else, we ought to treat these three men as teachers.

# 2

# F·R·I·E·N·D·S

## A WORK OF TRULY
## BEWITCHING PROPAGANDA

T HERE IS A LONGSTANDING DISTINC-
tion in the discipline of cultural criticism between
*fantasy* and *imagination* (incidentally, a distinction
deployed with great insight to the field of education by Maria
Montessori). "Fantasy," here, is not meant in the sense of the
artistic and literary genre. (In fact, some works of that sort of
fantasy—especially the "high fantasy" of J. R. R. Tolkien—are
among the best examples of *imaginative* achievement.) The
critical distinction between fantasy and imagination, on the
other hand, pertains to whether a given artistic work fosters
a better apprehension of reality or provides a mechanism for
intellectual and emotional departure from reality.

Imagination — not fantasy — is precisely what a child is
utilising in the act of play. The young boy who charges
round the garden with a wooden sword, slaying invisible
dragons and storming unseen citadels, is engaging in exactly
the sort of imitation of virtue that Aristotle proposes in the
*Nicomachean Ethics* as a precondition for habituating real
virtue. Imagination in the arts presents to the one on whom
it bestows its gifts a way of seeing things that creatively
illumines the world in which one actually lives. This is why,
despite what modern educationists will tell you, storytelling
and playing are the fundamental principles of good education
in early childhood; it is also why a rule-based, technique-
centred education, largely delivered through the medium
of virtual reality — widely promoted today as the best kind
of education — is the surest way to thwart young minds.

Unlike imagination, fantasy permits one to depart from

reality and take refuge in cheap consolations that cannot be found in this world and would wreck our world if they were here. Pornography is arguably the worst of such fantastical prisons. But there are less obvious sources of epistemic spell-casting that make engagement with reality difficult at best, and at worst impossible. The philosopher John Haldane, mentioned earlier in this volume, has pointed to the 1990 movie *Pretty Woman* as a good example of fantasy in this sense. In this story, a very wealthy man played by Richard Gere picks up a roadside prostitute played by Julia Roberts, asking her to drive him about because he's struggling to work the manual-drive car he's borrowing at the time. Later that night, they have sex. A romantic rollercoaster then ensues in which the hitherto money-driven man is transformed into an altruistic hero by the straightforward personality of his new companion, whom he showers with cash and for whom — after some drama — he eventually declares his love in a theatrical gesture involving a white limousine. The movie is pure trash from start to end, but it achieved remarkable success at the box office.

*Pretty Woman* presents a world that can tell you nothing about the one in which we actually live. It is, in the modern idiom, *escapism*. Surely no one is beyond redemption, but our nature being what it is, it's nonetheless commonly observed that even elementary relationships — like those between family and friends, and especially between spouses — are maintained by a lifetime of both tacit and deliberately cultivated virtue. Even then, such connections remain poised on the precipice of conflict, ever upheld by sacrifices and apologies. That a roadside prostitute who has known only abuse since childhood (personal experiences which Roberts' character discusses in the movie), has been sexually exploited for decades, physically attacked and degraded, and has likely acquired several substance-dependencies that only intensify the chaos of her life, could even come close to living the life portrayed in that film or forming the relationship therein is beyond credibility. The movie is a pernicious work of fantasy that utterly warps its viewers' conception of reality.

I have come to see such works of unreality as propaganda mechanisms of our progressivist regime, necessary to keep alive the fiction that whatever one's situation, history, behaviours, habits, ethical commitments, social standing, and so forth, there is always the pre-societal "authentic self" which can be emancipated through the moral and material conditions offered alone by the liberal regime of globalised late modernity. Gere's character is, if you like, the personification of that regime. He is driven only by the impulse to accumulate capital, and the ultimate corollary of such mammonian appetite is, apparently, spiritual enlightenment and redemption for everyone — without any need of repentance. Liberalism, in this sense, is itself a work of fantasy. At its core is the notion that I need not better understand reality and its conditions, but I need to free my *self* from that reality by the forces of Progress, that I may ultimately become that thing I know not what, to live in that society I have not seen.

According to liberal progressivism, the instrumentalization of science will get us to that future state of individualistic paradise, and the all-encompassing state will be the providential god that will steer us there. We needn't do anything more than enjoy being the beneficiaries of these forces of Progress that, it is said, increasingly unshackle us with each passing day. But this is quite clearly a fantasy. And to keep us believing the lie, a great, bewitching propaganda machine is required, which will tell us the stories that continually capture us from reality and place us in liberalism's fantasia.

There is perhaps no better example of such a work of propaganda than the American sitcom *Friends*. For a decade, from 1994 to 2004, it seemed as if everybody was watching *Friends* week in-week out. My parents, siblings, and I certainly did; then we bought the videos and re-watched the episodes. I'm not sure there was ever a greater work of liberal propaganda that was so influential in shaping the worldview of my generation. The script was brilliantly written, with a humorous remark at least every five seconds, and even a laugh-track to tell you when to be amused. The sitcom really was astonishingly popular (I remember the *Friends* pencil cases and water bottles that children would bring to school), and it remains the second highest grossing series of all time, just after the cartoon *The Simpsons*.

*Friends* has seen some backlash in recent years from the "woke" crowd, many of whom belong to Generation Z and are thus young enough to be encountering the sitcom for the first time. These youngsters have been scandalised at the lack of homosexual, trans, or black people in the cast. (This, of course, is the trouble with being in the vanguard of Progress: one soon finds oneself struggling to keep up.) Such "Wokerati" haven't recognised the truly revolutionary charm of *Friends* and how deeply saturated it is with the very anthropological and moral principles which they uphold. *Friends* helped to create a vision of adult behaviour and what flourishing in early adulthood looks like, without which "wokeness" today might have still been a weird, fringe subculture, rather than the shared ethic of our political and social elites.

If you are one of the cave-dwellers who isn't aware, there are six friends who together make up the leading characters in the sitcom. Ross and Monica are siblings and both secular Jews, completely disconnected from their religious heritage; Ross is considered the really brainy one of the group because he's a "sCiEnTiSt." Phoebe has a history of crime and homelessness, and is the only religious one of the group, being a practicing witch and New Ager; she is typified by her stupidity (apparently fitting for someone with any religious leanings). Chandler is the particularly witty and sarcastic one, whose father is a transvestite, homosexual cabaret performer in Las Vegas (Chandler's discomfort with his father's "identity" has caused outrage among some of *Friends'* recently acquired younger viewers). Rachel comes from a wealthy background and has an on-and-off relationship with Ross throughout the ten seasons. Joey is a struggling actor who, like Phoebe, is characterised by stupidity; he's a lapsed Catholic and a porn-addict, a disorder that the audience is meant to find both charming and comical.

According to the *Friends* fantasy, one can routinely sleep around; be incapable of establishing a stable relationship; develop a porn addiction; have a chaotic professional life, continually moving from job to job; irregularly turn up to work; contract multiple marriages; have children out of wedlock; be alienated from one's own offspring; have casual sex with those in your close friendship group; be conditioned by totally dysfunctional family units; actively develop an utterly vacuous, hedonistic approach to life, devoid of any overarching moral account of one's existence, and still live in a large apartment next to New York's Central Park, drink artisanal coffee all day, and never get a sexually transmitted infection or have an abortion.

*Friends* is American liberalism's version of one of China's communist theme parks: *just look at the lives we could all be living if we were really committed to the regime!* For many millennials, *Friends* provided the near-absolute blueprint of what a healthy early-adulthood might look like. Many of my school chums, following their university-provided lobotomies, moved to big cities and embarked on lives that imitated what *Friends* had offered as a vision of human flourishing, proceeding to plunge themselves into acute misery.

Liberalism promised to fulfil our lives by demoting all questions of flourishing and meaning to private, personal sentiment, with no claim on the public arena whatever. Liberalism has never, though, actually done this. It has offered an alternative account of human flourishing centred on the basest and most shallow commitments to specious emotions and the satiating of appetitive cravings. By so doing, it gave us a new religiosity with a whole set of new aspirations about how we should live and whom we should be. Liberalism has always been, then, a religious phenomenon, and it has always needed religious narratives to fill the imaginative faculties of us fools with the fantasies needed to becharm us. This is what *Friends* was all about. The regime gives us such narratives in a thousand ways through the pop-culture propaganda machine, declaring:

> Therefore, do not be anxious, saying, "What shall
> we eat?" or "What shall we drink?" or "What shall
> we wear?" For even conservatives seek after all
> these things, and the State knows that you need
> them all. But rather, seek first the authentic self
> and its moral emancipation, and all these things
> will be added to you.

Decades later, after much experience of sexual degradation,
superficial (virtual, even) "friendships," captivity by addiction,
economic disparity, rising debt, and family breakdown,
the attempt to conform our world to the liberal sitcom has
left us jaded. *Friends*-educated millennials are generally more
at home in virtual reality (or, unreality) than reality, they
struggle to make prudent professional decisions, are alarmingly
entitled, and have extremely unstable friendship groups
and sex lives. Millennials haven't just been unable to get the
large apartments next to Central Park, they won't even get
mortgages in the whole course of their lives. Trapped inside
the comedy, they've discovered it's nothing like its portrayal
on the television, and it's definitely not funny.

I'm a millennial, and for my part I do not have a television
for precisely the reason that I don't want a propaganda
machine of a regime I despise forming my worldview, let
alone that of my children. Thankfully my wife agrees. It
seems to me that this is the only way to outwit the regime at
the cultural level within the borders of the domestic sphere.
The moment my children had elementary attention capacities,
I read to them Kipling's *The Jungle Book*, Grahame's *The
Wind in the Willows*, Tolkien's entire Legendarium, and
countless stories from our ever-growing library of folktales.
As my sproglets grow, no doubt the challenge will also grow
of inducting them into a contra-modern, pro-traditional
worldview. At least, though, they will have some intuitive
grasp of the distinction between fantasy and imagination, and
that's more than can be said of most who stumble confusedly
in the darkness of our "enlightened" epoch.

# 3

# FOLK MUSIC AND DANCING
# WITH CHILDREN

M Y WIFE AND I WERE BOTH SHOCKED
and disturbed by our children's intolerance of classical music. We had always listened to classical
music, especially on car journeys or when lounging, ponder-
ingly, on the sofas in the evening. The greats—Beethoven,
Mozart, Bach, Handel, Schubert, Haydn, Debussy, Verdi,
Sibelius, Elgar, Vaughan Williams—often accompanied us.
If we were feeling especially merry, Vivaldi would sound
out. We sometimes solemnly sat to sacred pieces, especially
Tallis, Byrd, Palestrina, Victoria, and Allegri. The moderns
sometimes appeared: Messiaen, Tavener, MacMillan . . . Then
the children began to declare their disgruntlement. Their
incapacity to endure some chamber music or a work of
polyphony was disheartening.

One thing was clear, though: we were not going to play
pop music. Pop music, generally speaking, is evil. It debases
the soul and makes people stupid. Pop music has become
increasingly corrupting over the decades since its emergence.
And now, each pop song appears to consist solely of a three-
and-a-half minute intro. The beat goes on and on, and the
occasional abstract platitudinous remark is sung in an elec-
tronically manipulated voice about some base emotional
impulse, and then the beat continues. One sits there, waiting
for the song to actually take off, and it never does. In this
way, pop music reflects the modern mind, which is always
on the verge of possessing the utopian epoch, marching
forth to abstractions uttered as promises . . . but it never
actually takes off.

A possible alternative would have been to play *early* pop:
Bing Crosby, Frank Sinatra, Dean Martin, even Elvis Presley.

This would be, though, like trying to avoid the corruption of the soul by just slowing down the corrupting process. It's all the same rubbish as the noises we produce today, but it just sits upstream a little. Perhaps the most terrible thing about pop music, and early stuff is as guilty as our current clamours, is that it relies on abstractions — isolated emotional states, usually emanating from chaotic appetitive impulses — described in something pretending to be a song. In this way, pop music — dislodged from *the particular* and relocated in the realm of abstractions — attempts to belong to everywhere and to everyone at once. It is a universal kind of music, and by attempting to belong to everywhere it belongs to nowhere. Listening to pop music, much like the rest of modernity, marks an education in unreality, which is no education at all.

What music, then, were we to play on long journeys in the car or in our home that the children would find tolerable? We started playing folk music. Not modern folk-pop, but *real* folk music. We found recordings of old English folk songs, and in the car we would sing along to *The Lincolnshire Poacher, Because I Were Shy, Jack Hall, The Barkshire Tragedy,* and good old bawdy numbers like The Raggle Taggle Gypsy and *Gently Johnny my Jingalo*. We learned the words to *John Barleycorn, Drink to me only with Thine Eyes, The Derby Ram, John Anderson, Sovay, As I Roved Out, Star of County Down,* and some good old hunting songs like *Tally Ho! My Fine Sportsmen* and *John Peel*. We discovered the great figures at the heart of the mid-20th century folk revival (before it was hijacked and ruined by the pop production industry) like Luke Kelly, Martin Carthy, and The Chieftains. To our delight, our kids loved it all.

An astonishing feature of all authentic folk music is its antipathy towards abstractions. The songs are generally stories about a particular community, in a particular place, going through a particular event at a particular time, and the particular individuals or couples that underwent it. Folk music is invariably rooted in the concrete reality of life. Take, for example, the following opening lyrics of *The Lincolnshire Poacher*, a rustic song from the mid-18th century:

> When I was bound apprentice in famous Lincolnshire
> Full well I served my master for nigh on seven years
> Till I took up to poaching as you shall quickly hear
> Oh, 'tis my delight on a shiny night in the season of
> the year.
>
> As me and my companions was setting out a snare
> 'Twas then we spied the gamekeeper, for him we didn't
> care
> For we can wrestle and fight, my boys, and jump from
> anywhere
> Oh, 'tis my delight on a shiny night in the season of
> the year.

We know, within two verses, that this is a story about a man who was an indentured servant, not far off a slave, living in Lincolnshire, who was fettered in this way for nearly seven years. He clearly broke the contract of his indentured servitude and fled his master, soon being without the proper means to feed himself. Hence, he took up poaching, venturing out in the evenings to snare hares. He was joined in this highly illegal activity by others, no doubt with equally unfortunate histories, with whom he had to carefully avoid the gamekeepers of the land on which they were poaching. Gamekeepers, incidentally, are a respected but rough breed. Clearly, for this young man and his friends, encounters with such keepers in the past necessitated learning how to fight and wrestle. All this we learn within a minute of the song beginning.

Now, compare the lyrics above to the opening two verses of a 2014 song entitled *Bang Bang* by the pop-singers Jessie J, Ariana Grande, and Nicki Minaj:

> She got a body like an hourglass
> But I can give it to you all the time
> She got a booty like a Cadillac
> But I can send you into overdrive, oh.
> You've been waiting for that

Step on up, swing your bat
See, anybody could be bad to you
You need a good girl to blow your mind, yeah.

One can imagine these words written in excrement on the
cell wall of a sectioned psychopath. What, though, can we
learn from these lines? Well, there is a woman — we do not
know who she is — who is characterised by an unfortunate
body-shape, being compared here to an egg timer fastened
to a large American car (an image my imagination strains
but fails to form). Verse two is even more cryptic, but I am
informed that "bat" in this case refers to the penis belonging
to the man to whom the lyrics are addressed; the rest seems
to require arcane decipherment in order to bring to the fore
the complex sexual psychology being deployed, for which I
am unqualified.

In truth, what we have in this pop song is utter rubbish,
produced to ensnare people. In the first example — that of
the old folk song — we have a story, deeply bound up with
something real, contextual, cultural, and historical, which
is also entertaining and memorable. My family and I have
many a time sat around the table after breakfast on a Saturday morning and sang our favourite folk songs together.
The children have an amazing capacity for picking up the
lyrics, and it's a joy to listen to them. On the other hand,
it is difficult to imagine a situation in which my children
could suitably encourage me to join them in a sing-song of
*Bang Bang*, whose content is evidently so esoteric that it
took three "artists" to come up with it.

My wife and I were confirmed in our low-cultural response
to our children's intolerance of classical music last summer
whilst holidaying in north Devon. Having spent the afternoon below the enchanting Tintagel Castle — a hallowed
place wrapped in Arthurian legend — paddling about at
the beach under the gaze of Merlin's cliff-face carving, we
hopped into the car and headed back to our lodgings. As
we wound down the narrow country roads of Cornwall and

drew close to the Devonshire border, the children began to complain that they were hungry.

We pulled into a rural village, at the top of whose square was a thatched pub, The Green Dragon. In we walked and were greeted with smiles and head-nods. "May we have a menu?" I asked. The lady behind the bar replied, "We're serving sausages and mash tonight." "Four sausages and mash then, please."

The pub was serving one kind of meal and one kind of ale. So, that made ordering a simple affair. As we finished our food (which was exactly what we all needed after a day of walking on Cornwall's north coastal hills and swimming in the sea for hours), we watched through the window as a large yellow van pulled into the village square. The back doors of the van swung open, and out jumped ten Morris dancers. I will never forget the look on my children's faces as they watched what appeared to be a gang of oversized hobbits leap out and spring about with a wooden horse. Soon, the villagers had all come out of their cottages to enjoy the spectacle. We ate up, picked up our pints — lemonades for the little ones — and wandered out to watch the Morris dancers.

There we sat in the twilight for the next hour or so watching the wonderful dances and listening to that old music that appeared to have the sounds of the centuries encased within it. The children clapped and danced around too. My affectivity, so warped and darkened by decades of exposure to modernity, could hardly cope with the wholesomeness of it all. Our children, formed in their aesthetic attachments by hundreds of hours of folk music, listened and danced and claimed the whole event as their own. This was, they judged, *their* culture and *their* music.

My children, though, are not Cornish. They're barely English. But my wife and I have enough sense to know that there is no such thing as a "citizen of the world." The only true belonging is local belonging, and we always knew that the imperative before us in raising our children was to induct them into a cultural inheritance that they could call theirs. They couldn't, we decided, live as aliens in this world. Indeed, the minimum we could give them was the experience of being at home in the world. Folk music has been a major part of teaching the children, implicitly and by habit, that history, place, culture, and real things matter. In short, folk music helps to purify us of the rationalism that is in the very air we breathe in the modern world.

When the energy is low, or irritability begins to cover the domestic sphere with its dark mantle, we put on some folk music and dance together around the house. I scoop my children up into my arms and leap around, singing at the top of my voice. They clap and laugh and sing along, and for a brief moment all the stupidity and perversion of the modern world, for us at least, disappears. It is quite likely that, in a few decades if not before, when I lie on my deathbed and make my final confession, begging for the Lord to save me by the merits of His passion and death, I will not wonder why I didn't write more books or publish more academic papers. I will probably wonder why I didn't spend more time dancing with my wife and children to old folk songs — that this is a cliché makes it no less true.

# 4

# ON NOT LOOKING AWFUL

BEFORE WE CHOSE TO HOME-EDUCATE our children, it was more often than not my job to drop them off at their school in the morning. I found it very difficult, even remotely, to respect the other dads I saw standing outside the school gate. Most of them looked like overgrown kids themselves. Typically, the fathers wore track-suit bottoms—what in the U.S. are called "sweatpants"—and t-shirts, hooded jumpers, and trainers. Acceptable, perhaps, if you're off to a workout, but these men were off to the office. They looked awful. I would look upon these men, most of whom were middle-class and white-collar workers, and I'd think, *what a bunch of scruffs*.

When I was a schoolboy, had my father turned up at the school gate dressed like that, I would have asked him henceforth to remain in the car. In fact, I am quite shocked by the speed with which we in the West have become a people who look awful, almost all the time. My concern here is with the turnout of men, but frankly, women are doing no better. In the winter, women now seem to walk about in huge sleeping bags with sleeves, looking like great sacks of potatoes. In the summer, they forget they possess a wardrobe at all, wandering only in undergarments. I always thought leggings were exclusively undergarments until I was disabused of this assumption some years ago. Throughout the warmer months, women took to wearing leggings and crop-tops with nothing else. The latest fashion, it has not escaped my notice, is for the synthetic fabric of the leggings to disappear up between the cheeks of the woman's rear, leaving the imagination with nothing.

Now, I can appreciate the well-toned curvature of spandex-coated buttocks as much as the next man, but the fact is that the world now looks awful, largely because there's a lot of us walking about in it and *we* all look awful.

I have seen black-and-white photographs of unemployed people during the Great Depression in the 1930s; desperate for work and achingly hungry, they nonetheless dressed themselves handsomely. Only a century ago, from the shopkeeper and farmworker to the factory owner and landed squire, a basic sense of presentation was considered essential to being a functioning human being in a functioning human society, even when it wasn't functioning very well at all. Woollen jacket and trousers, a hat, collared shirt, necktie, and leather shoes were not considered the garb of the wealthy alone, but the elementary pieces of any man's attire.

Now, I am not calling for a return to such clothing, though that wouldn't be the worst option. As it happens, I do not much like suits. I think matching jacket and trousers tends to look too much like pyjamas, which is the only other outfit I can think of for which a man wears a matching top and bottoms. I also think that the suit has contributed to what a friend of mine calls the "dictatorship of grey" — his name for all that is modern. The suit is in many ways the garb of an egalitarian society, wherein everyone — whatever their actual status or social position — must walk about in the same pair of PJs, with the only bit of flair being whether you opt for blue or grey and striped or checked. Just look at the glorious and multifarious outfits of Renaissance Italy or Regency England, and you can see how grey everything has since become. Nonetheless, if our decomposing modernity's suggested getup is "active wear," then give me a society of suited men any day.

I stress that only a century ago it was the norm for ordinary and average people not to look awful because, when I point out how awful people look today, it is only a matter of time before I am accused of "snobbery" and "privilege." As for my "snobbery," *I* deem it snobbish to dismiss others as those who can do no better than look like trash. My vexation with the awfulness of how those around me dress does not come from looking down my nose at them, but rather from my belief that they need not look awful at all. They look awful out of choice, and it is a choice I treat with disdain. And if I *am* snobbish when it comes to dressing, that is a snobbishness in which I want all others to join me. In fact, my snobbery is a very inclusive snobbery. And in my defence, I quote Sir Roger Scruton's description of the great Monsignor Alfred Gilbey:

> Even if you take his sartorial perfectionism, his clubbability, his Beerbohmian zest for social nuances, his lifelong addiction to hunting with hounds, his antiquarianism and his love of the old England of country house and Trollopian intrigue — even if you take all this and, discounting his constant visits among the poor, the sick and the dying, and the universal reach of his friendship, make it add up in some way to snobbery, then that only shows that snobbery can be close to sanctity.[1]

A snobbery that wants to elevate others and rejoice in their aesthetic successes, and not one that seeks to crush or disparage others, is, in my view, a holy snobbery. That is the snobbery I seek to habituate, and it is a virtue that I invite others to cultivate. And as for "privilege," I can only say that one can — I know from experience — not look awful on a very tight budget. Note that I do not claim that one can look *good*, though I hasten to add that, in fact, one *can* look good on a tight budget. Given that at present the norm, however, is to look awful, I'm setting the bar at reaching the negative accomplishment of merely not looking awful.

When it comes to not looking awful on a tight budget, charity shops are your friends. In the early years of my marriage, when my wife and I were very poor and every penny counted, in our attempt not to look awful, we would travel to the wealthy parts of London and visit those locations'

---

[1] Roger Scruton, *Gentle Regrets: Thoughts from a Life* (London: Continuum, 2005), 70.

charity shops. We found that tucked away were charity shops in Mayfair and Kensington where one could purchase beautiful, high-quality, well-cut clothing that had recently been discarded after one or two wears by very rich people. These items could be bought up for a tiny fraction of the original price, and thus it was possible not to look awful by just practising the ancient art of gleaning with regard to the wealthy's hand-me-downs.

Now, when such clothes do eventually wear thin, or the seams become loose, or the cuffs begin to fray, there is a simple solution: needle and thread. I have very few clothes that I have not patched up or stitched up. You can double the life of a garment by putting in a stitch here or there without delay. True, once you've done this quite a few times on a single item of clothing, it starts to look a little trampish. On the other hand, that may not be a bad thing. In the UK, at least, there are two types of people who traditionally dress like tramps: tramps and aristocrats. Quite likely, as long as you have the occasional shower and aren't constantly drunk, people will just think you belong to the latter. In fact, come to think of it, forget the shower and drink as much as you like, and people will perhaps have more reason to think you belong to the latter.

I do not believe it is any cheaper to buy t-shirts, hooded jumpers, fluorescent puffer coats, and all that garbage than to go to a charity shop and buy second-hand but very nice clothing. On a tight budget, by being creative and visiting such shops, you can deck out your entire wardrobe in a few months without breaking the bank, and at the end of it, you won't look awful.

As things stand, whether you're in Boston, Birmingham, Bucharest, or Bombay, everyone seems to be wearing the same tracksuits and NY baseball caps. The universalisation of the worst aspects of American anti-culture has been a catastrophe. From Washington to Sydney, everyone's in the same American sweatpants made in the same Asian sweatshops. The world, which used to be home to innumerable cultures with countless sartorial expressions, has all fallen under the global dictatorship of grey, and now everyone looks awful. To combat this effect, visit charity shops and buy the beautiful clothes of recently deceased people who belonged to a generation that understood how to dress nicely.

There are two very rudimentary reasons why it is necessary to take care not to look awful. The first and less important reason is that dressing nicely conveys to yourself that you possess a certain dignity, that you ought to be taken seriously, and that you are a grown-up. The second, and much more vital reason, is that by dressing nicely, you indicate that you respect others. The person who dresses nicely says by his outfit, and he says it to every person he meets: "Look, I have made an effort, because you're worth that effort, and I wouldn't want to look awful while we're spending time together, even if it's only for a passing moment." Dressing nicely, then, is one of the key aspects of having *manners*, which is a somewhat Victorian way of saying, *of being in right relation with others*, and it's being in right relation with others that makes you fully a person. Thus, this is not as frivolous a topic as it may seem at first glance.

This brings me to the three sartorial basics that every Western man ought to know and around which he ought to construct his outfits. To be clear, I am no natty dresser, and I do not claim to have any authority when it comes to dressing well or even properly. I am merely someone who strives, as best he can, not to look utterly awful, and I invite others to do the same. The three sartorial basics are: a lapelled jacket, a collared shirt, and leather shoes. That's it. It's that simple.

Yes, it is *very* simple indeed, but the variety is almost endless. You can wear a cotton, linen, tweed, moleskin, corduroy, velvet, or whatever jacket. You can go with whatever colour or pattern shirt you like. Trousers, creased or not, could be chinos, corduroys, denim if you really must, or whatever you fancy. Shoes might be black or brown, Oxfords or Derbys, brogue or plain, suede or polished. It's all up to you. If you're invited somewhere, as long as you've built your outfit on the foundation of the three sartorial basics, all you need to do is put on a necktie, and you'll look fine. If the event turns out to be more casual than you expected, lose the necktie, and you'll still look fine. Either way, you won't look awful. In warmer months, opt for a short sleeve collared shirt. In colder months, add a jumper, gilet, or waistcoat under your jacket. Not looking awful, it turns out, is so very easy.

Once you've learned not to look awful, you'll discover that dressing is a little like poetry, in that one can only break or bend the rules effectively and with panache once one actually knows the rules and is experienced in applying them. So, then, break the rules: opt for a collarless shirt with a linen jacket in the summer, switch your laced shoes to Chelsea boots or loafers, or do whatever you like. You see, now that you no longer look awful, you're a free man. And hopefully, you will use your freedom wisely and never look awful again.

## ❧ AFTERWORD ❧

A S AN APOSTATE FROM THE CONTEM-
porary ideological paradigm, and now an Anglo-
Catholic convert of a few years standing—although
I'm not sure one "converts" from nihilism, but rather runs
screaming towards meaning—I can't compete with Sebastian
Morello on the finer points of liturgy. Yet *Unto the Ages of
Ages* is a profoundly open and welcoming text to anyone who
has arrived—from very different starting points—at a similar
diagnosis of what's wrong with the modern world, but also,
and vitally, on a set of ideas about what to do about it.

There are many fine arguments in Morello's text. I'm particularly convinced by his beautifully made argument about
how the British are firmly embedded in the revolutionary
paradigm, and yet how "progressive" (destructive) ideas have
been sold to the people time and time again under the brand
of "Conservatism." "We English," Morello puts it, "adopt
everything that is procured by revolutions, but we do so
without the revolutions."

It has long struck me that conservatism, at least as practised
by the UK political party of that name, has little to do with
preservation, conservation, tradition, or anything remotely
organic, be it with the land or its people. Morello reinforces
this impression, and, following his mentor Roger Scruton,
notes that conservatism is above all about love: "True conservatism always seeks to unify, affirm, treasure, understand,
*conserve*. It belongs to the impulses of the revolutionary to
divide, tear down, protest, reject, repudiate, destroy."

Rather than the faux conservatism to which we've grown
accustomed, Morello proposes not only an unapologetic
Christianity — "The role of a Christian in the face of such
corruption of reality is to reject it outright and undergo the
hard slog of retrieving a pre-modern mind and heart" — but
also a "right-wing ecumenism." He writes: "I want to suggest
that the members of the baptised, whatever their religious

divisions, work together to undermine and ultimately destroy the progressivist supremacy that dominates the West, recognising that it marks a settlement incompatible with even a basic Biblical worldview." No doubt he is right that such collaboration between Christians is pressing indeed.

Where do we find ourselves today? Morello provides, perhaps surprisingly, a sympathetic explanation for the excesses of progressivism. I say sympathetic because his starting point is profound and often overlooked, namely that there is no such thing as the "non-religious," and that "secularism" is the name today for a "kind of ontological schizophrenia" in which "the secular denies its own essence and repudiates that which comes from without for the achievement of its end." Secularism is, he writes, "a pathology, a fiction, and what it claims as true will never be brought into reality." Furthermore, "[t]he only reason why we assume that the political arena *can* be secular or religiously neutral is because in the West we were until comparatively recently a Christian people."

Morello argues that progressivism is, in its own way, "an expression of a very deep and noble religious need." Late-stage progressivism, Morello argues, stems from

> a deeply religious attempt to provide a rapidly fragmenting community with a sense of common purpose . . . it has its own theology; its moral decrees; its sacrificial victims; its proselytizers; a highly effective inquisition; an exegetical methodology for interpreting history; an index of forbidden books; its iconography — especially the "selfie," that frozen avatar of the disembodied 'authentic self'; it has its saints and martyrs; its doctrine of healthcare and safety as the topmost ethical values; its idolatry of technologies as the angelic mediators that will bring about a new heaven and a new earth; and it promotes the LGBTQ+ movement as the highest religious expression, with its public processions, flags and banners, and a liturgical year complete with holy days and months of festivities.

In this sense, progressivism is a desperate last bid to ward off nihilism, just as the behaviour of many during the COVID lockdowns of 2020–21 was perhaps indicative of a desperate bid negatively to shore up a dying idea of the public (though let's not forgive too quickly). Hence, paradoxically, there are some glimmers of hope here.

Morello rightly observes that there is both a profound and superficial religious dimension at stake, only with all the zeal and none of the transcendence and social realism that Christianity offers: no forgiveness, no acceptance of the shared reality that we are all sinners, no possibility of redemption, and so on. As a "bad person" from the standpoint of this late modern worldview, one feels at times as if one's soul is being investigated with a magnifying glass by someone who just knows that a black spot is already there, but is not also in them.

There are three core arguments I want to take from Morello's essays and extend, by way of René Girard, Christopher Lasch, and Ivan Illich:

1. Humanity is fundamentally religious.
2. The dominant contemporary religion is science, or scientistic, the fantasy of progress without end, bodies without limits, and so on.
3. That there are better and worse religions, false and true liturgies.

One significant dimension of progressivism is summarised by James G. Williams in his introduction to Girard's *I See Satan Fall Like Lightning* as "victimism." Williams writes that "Victimism uses the ideology of concern for victims to gain political or economic or spiritual power. One claims victim status as a way of gaining an advantage or justifying one's behaviour."

Alongside this insight is the Girardian idea that Williams brings to the fore of the "single victim mechanism," i.e. scapegoating as "the community's unconscious way of converging on someone it blames for its troubles." This is the work of Satan who, for Girard, is the accuser. Unavoidable mimetic rivalry and envy generate this need for a scapegoat. And we see versions of this phenomenon everywhere around us today, with individuals or groups rushing to take the place of Christ. The more literary versions might talk about vulnerability or precarious lives, and so on, but they all solve the need for victims by either inventing new ones — never-ending according to the scientific model of progress — or dividing humanity up into victims and oppressors.

In modernity, law replaces morality and contracts replace covenants, but the fundamental solution presented by Christ's death and resurrection, and any mature engagement with the problem of original sin, is obscured. The choice between nihilism or God is both never resolved and resolved over and over through new victims and new scapegoats. History becomes retroactively conditioned as purely Manichean and there is no history of virtue to draw upon, even the frag-mented one that Alisdair MacIntyre describes in *After Virtue*.

Christopher Lasch's argument in *The True and Only Heaven* (from 1991), is that today's idea of progress is not so much a secularized version of the Christian belief in providence, whose imitators he suggests collapsed following the murderous and totalitarian regimes of the early and mid-20th century, but rather a post-utopian idea. So, the idea of progress has certainly persisted, but not as a non-religious version of Christian millenarianism. As Lasch puts it: "not the promise of a secular utopia that would bring history to a happy ending but the promise of steady improvement with no foreseeable ending at all." For Lasch, the idea of progress never "rested mainly on the promise of an ideal society," but rather "the modern conception of history is utopian only in its assumption that modern history has no foreseeable conclusion."

For Lasch, nothing is certain except "the imminent obso-lescence of all our certainties — our scientific theories, our technology, our artistic styles and schools, our philosophies, our political ideals, our fashions." Yet, there is a simultaneous persistence at work:

impermanence appears to assure a certainty continuity in its own right when conceived as an extension of the self-correcting procedures of scientific discovery, which allow the scientific enterprise as a whole to flourish in spite of the constant revision of particular findings. A social order founded on science, with its unnerving but exhilarating expansion of our intellectual horizons, seems to have achieved a kind of immortality undreamed of by earlier civilisations.

Only science, we suppose, "is immortal." "Trust the science," we might say. What choice do we have? As Morello notes, "we think that because we have iPhones, we must be morally superior to our forebears. Thus, we believe we must accept the moral dogmas of modernity, or it might seem like ingratitude for modern medicine and telephones."

It is worth exploring the differentiation between an immanentised quasi- or inverted religious idea of progress and a scientific one. We can see how a scientific idea of progress without end, without finality, in a perfect nation (with all the bloodshed that involves), is playing out: the fantasy that science will "save us" is common to both the so-called Left and Right, whether it be the delusion that the body has no limits, or that space is the telos for humanity, or that we can avoid suffering through technology, or that we can solve all the problems we have created through technology with more technology. There is an endless attack on the limits of human nature, or even a denial of any such limits. We observe the creation of new subjects and patients, and we end up somewhere between a spreadsheet entry, a fungible node in a weightless technical vision, and a lifelong dependency on the state. In an article entitled "Imago DEI: Human Nature, Technology, and the Progress Dilemma" the social critic Mary Harrington has put this in contemporary terms:

> conservatives on both Christian and modernist sides must seek common cause in disavowing any politics of technology that extends... [the] legacy

[of technology] to repudiating an account of the
human. The endpoint of such a repudiation will
inevitably be the bio-leftism of *imago DEI*.

What is this idea of man as the instantiation of *imago DEI* —
of diversity, equity, and inclusion? Harrington defines him
as "a protean plurality governed only by its willingness to see
the dissolution of all difference as a good in its own right."

Lasch was writing during the high point of a certain
rationalism, namely the New Atheist movement, which
has since somewhat succumbed to its own hubris, with
many of its proponents defending a certain Christian culture
and legacy, if not belief. Nonetheless, it is not paradoxical
to say that science remains the dominant religion of the
west, whether we are talking about transhumanism, or AI,
or the conquering of the stars. When Elon Musk and the
technophilic Right talk about "Mars," they likely mean the
God of war, less than the planet. What is being proposed is
the domination of space by technology for the purposes of
war, communications, media, and surveillance. "Mars" is an
aspiration that taps into the Promethean element of man's
desires, but also invokes bloody ambitions at the global level.

To try to understand the depth of our deracination, I want
now to focus on institutions and literacy, via the work of
Ivan Illich (1926–2002), a sort of renegade anarcho-Catholic.
(Hopefully the connections to Morello's essays will be clear
to the reader.) In a late interview, Illich said the following:

> We are in a situation in which the disembodiment
> of the I-Thou relationship has led into a mathe-
> matization, an algorithmization, which supposedly
> is experienced.... I think many people have very
> reasonably withdrawn from trying to improve the
> social agencies and organizations for which only
> twenty years they felt responsible. They know
> that all they can do is to try, by negative criteria,
> to diminish the impact and the hold of this idea
> on their milieu, in order to be increasingly free
> to behave an-archically as human beings who do

> not act for the sake of the city, but because they
> have received the ability to respond as a gift from
> the other.[1]

Is the institution ultimately tied to the metropolis? Are
there no institutions in the countryside? The human, and
what ultimately makes us human—namely interpersonal
relatedness with the other—is here opposed to the institution: you cannot humanise an institution, you can only
behave against it, in the name of the present, in relation to
the other. The institution, despite being composed of people,
is, for Illich, ultimately inhuman, or will likely become so.

What are we to make of such a provocation today, when
we are not even sure which institutions we are members of?
We are in a miasma of belonging, as an endless stream of
numbers, memberships, passwords; as workers or students,
participants in countless organisations and arrangements that
do not even necessarily announce themselves as such. We rely
upon, or are coerced into participation in, institutions all the
time—the major ones: schooling, healthcare; but the shadow
ones too, the ones that present themselves as free choices:
politics, economics, marriage. And beneath them, language,
ideology, technologies, even the alphabet itself (about which
more shortly). We are all institutionalised. Churches and
cathedrals are treated by many first and foremost as aesthetic
and historic phenomena, not living traditions. It is quaint
to belong to a "parish" when internet space exists. And yet,
let us not fail to observe the growing desire for Christianity
and the Church.

It is interesting that even in the late 1990s, when these
interviews with Cayley were undertaken, Illich talked of the
"mathematization" and the "algorithmization" of things and
the "disembodiment" of the I-Thou relationship. It goes
without saying that these tendencies have reached levels
today that I'm not sure even Illich could have predicted. The

---

[1]  Ivan Illich, in conversation with David Cayley, "Across the Watershed,"
in *The Rivers North of the Future: The Testament of Ivan Illich, as Told
to David Cayley* (Toronto: House of Anansi, 2005).

institution necessarily exists beyond the present, and against it. It exists against spontaneity and unpredictability. While institutions are composed of people, gradually people start to become bearers of the institution as well, thus reproducing institutional values in human form. Most institutions start out with identifiable and often worthy aims and values. Many institutions become ossified and even start to work against their core principles. This tendency is summed up in a classical phrase to which Illich recurrently returns: *corruptio optimi pessima* — the corruption of the best is the worst. Schooling ceases to be about learning and becomes about other things: policing, regulating, training children for the economy, promoting normative ideas. Medicine ceases to preserve health and begins to encourage dependency on pills, and so on. The artistic institutions cease to celebrate creativity but reward adherence to a narrow range of ideological commitments.

This is not to say there are not counter-institutions or "good" institutions: certainly, the less a contemporary institution succumbs to the worsening impulse, the stronger it is. We might begin with Morello's help to draw up a vision of counter-institutions: the family, the Church, the inherited and organic traditions. It is not enough, though, merely to recognise them. One must actively participate in all of these things! So, how do we break with the long-standing techno-scientific paradigm and return to life?

In the 1988 work *ABC: The Alphabetisation of the Popular Mind*, Illich and his co-author Barry Sanders write the following:

> The techniques that have constituted alphabetic writing — consonants, vowels, breaks between words, paragraphs, titles — developed historically to become what they are today. Certain constructs that cannot exist without reference to the alphabet — thought and language, lie and memory, translation, and particularly the self — developed parallel to these writing techniques. If these categories

had a historical beginning, they can also come
to an end. Our keen awareness of literacy as a
historic construction whose first emergence we
can describe deepens our sense of responsibility
to preserve it. Standing firmly on the terra of
literacy, we can see two epistemological chasms.
One of these chasms cuts us off from the domain
of orality. The other, which moves like smog to
engulf us, equates letters with bits of information,
degrading reading and writing.

From the perspective offered by Illich and Sanders, the
alphabet can be seen as one of the first and most powerful
technologies (we are all creatures of the text) that leads to
systems and codes. As Illich and Sanders elsewhere note,
alluding to George Orwell, "We see Newspeak as a cipher
for something that is now called "interpersonal communication," for the belief that the terms by which we describe
the operations of computers are fit to tell what is going on
between you and me. By Newspeak we mean one particular
way of thinking and speaking about language — an approach
or an attitude that treats language as a system and a code."
In short, we are all becoming encoded. Such an erosion of
the human, however, is not a pre-determined inevitability.

What then of reality, being, nature, physis? In 1988, the
French sociologist and philosopher Jean Baudrillard suggested that:

Simulation is no longer that of a territory, a ref-
erential being or a substance. It is the generation
by models of a real without origin or reality: a
hyperreal.... It is no longer a question of imitation, nor of reduplication, nor even of parody. It
is rather a question of substituting signs of the
real for the real itself; that is, an operation to
deter every real process by its operational double,
a metastable, programmatic, perfect descriptive
machine which provides all the signs of the real
and short-circuits all its vicissitudes.

We are in the age of the "perfect descriptive machine," in which many contemporary institutions participate. We can see this above all in the reduction to "identity" of what has otherwise been merely organic being and belonging (sex, place, etc.). Against this, we must defend that which doesn't "work," which isn't a machine, which is not efficient, which is anti- or de-institutionalising (institutionalising, at least, in the problematic sense I have explicated above). We need to protect all that is organic, spontaneous, relational, strange, poetic, and that has a genuine history, which we might call *tradition*. As Morello put it with regard to a local public garden near to his home:

> The garden is also completely pointless. Or rather, it has no point beyond itself. It contains within itself its own purpose. Thus, it is one of the most important things in the town, for whilst most things are *means*, this garden is an *end*.

The course of modernity has hit a crisis point of no return. This crisis point has revealed that the abstractions — equality, universality, and the DEI updates — as well as multiculturalism and globalism and so on, are undone by the revenge of reality, despite the best efforts of our abstraction magicians to cast particular spells over us. The more *place* is dismantled, the more it will return. I think it is ultimately impossible to destroy the reality of what it means to live human lives, but that does not mean that we don't have a tough collective struggle before us. As Morello puts it: "recovery from the curse [of modernity] will largely rely on the nostalgic impulse." His essays here are a serious diagnosis and a joyful vision of the world into which we've been thrown, and what now must be saved.

Dr. Nina Power
*London*
*March 2025*

# INDEX OF NAMES

Aligehri, Dante, xviii, 56
Alacoque, St. Margaret Mary, 78
Austin, J. L., 112

de Beauvoir, Simone, 84
Bede, xvii
Bourgeois, Charles, 38
Briggs, William M., 123–124
Bugnini, Annibale, 70
Burke, Edmund, xvi–xvii, xxvi, xxxi, 8, 13, 15, 27, 29n3, 65–66, 74, 77, 85, 125–126, 128, 130, 139, 141 144

Cameron, David, xxviii, 40, 68
King Charles I, xxv, 11,
Chateaubriand, François-René, 10, 27, 130
Chaucer, Geoffrey, xvii
Chesterton, G. K., xvii, xxi, 130
Cromwell, Oliver, 11, 65
de Condillac, Étienne, 127
de Coulanges, Numa Fustel, 101
Curtis, Richard, xxvii

Davidson, John Daniel, 129–131, 133–134
Davos Jacobins, 69
Dawson, Christopher, xiii
Disraeli, Benjamin, 5, 8–9, 26
Dooley, Mark, 29n2, 101
Dryden, John, 12

Eliot, T. S., xiii, 56, 130

Girard, René, 165
Goethe, 56

Hailsham, Viscount, 89, 91
Haldane, John, 119–120, 146
Harari, Youval, 112

Harrington, Mary, xx, 111–116, 167–168
Hobbes, Thomas, 6, 113

Illich, Ivan, 165, 168–171

Kim Jong II, 23
King Henry VIII, xxviii, 71, 77
Kirk, Russell, xiii, 130
Keble, Reverend John, 5

Lasch, Christopher, 165–166, 168
Lewis, C. S., xiii, 81
Locke, John, 20–21, 66, 113–115,

de Maistre, Joseph, xvi, xxix, xxxii, 7, 61, 81, 125–127, 141
Montessori, Maria, 145
Queen Mary I, 71–72
Moreno, Gabriel García, 77
Musk, Elon, 168

Nero, xxiii
Newman, John Henry, xvi–xvii, xxiii, 5, 11–12, 73, 126, 130, 132
del Noce, Augusto, 140

Paul, St., xxiii, 24, 79–80
Peel, Robert, 10
Peter, St., xxiii, xxiv
Peterson, Jordan, 32, 95, 99
Pius V, Pope, 71
Pius IX, Pope, 72, 74
Pope, Alexander, 123
Pugin, Augustus, 72

Rilke, Rainer Maria, xviii
Ruth, 32, 42

Sack, James J., 11
Schwab, Klaus, 69

Scruton, Roger, xiii, xx, 28–33, 40, 62, 89, 100–101n1, 130–131, 159, 163
Socrates, 18
Solovyov, Vladimir, 142–144
Spaemann, Robert, 4
Starmer, Sir Kier, 35
Storck, Thomas, 21

Tallis, Raymond, 30
Taylor, Charles, xxii

Tennyson, Alfred, 33–34
Tolkien, J. R. R., xiv, xviii, 145, 150
Trump, Donald, 57

Vervaeke, John, 61

Weinstein, Bret, 124
William of Ockham, 64
Williams, Ralph Vaughan, 56, 151
Wycliff, John, 64